Study Guide for

# Ferraro's Cultural Anthropology

**Study Guide for**

# Ferraro's Cultural Anthropology
## An Applied Perspective
## Third Edition

**Mary Ann Medlin**
**Barber Scotia College**

**West/Wadsworth**
I⊤P® An International Thomson Publishing Company

Belmont, CA • Albany, NY • Bonn • Boston • Cincinnati • Detroit • Johannesburg • London
Madrid • Melbourne • Mexico City • New York • Paris • Singapore • Tokyo • Toronto • Washington

Printed in the United States of America
1  2  3  4  5  6  7  8  9  10

For more information, contact Wadsworth Publishing Company, 10 Davis Drive, Belmont, CA 94002, or electronically at http://www.thomson.com/wadsworth.html

International Thomson Publishing Europe
Berkshire House 168-173
High Holborn
London, WC1V 7AA, England

International Thomson Editores
Campos Eliseos 385, Piso 7
Col. Polanco
11560 México D.F. México

Thomas Nelson Australia
102 Dodds Street
South Melbourne 3205
Victoria, Australia

International Thomson Publishing Asia
221 Henderson Road
#05-10 Henderson Building
Singapore 0315

Nelson Canada
1120 Birchmount Road
Scarborough, Ontario
Canada M1K 5G4

International Thomson Publishing Japan
Hirakawacho Kyowa Building, 3F
2-2-1 Hirakawacho
Chiyoda-ku, Tokyo 102, Japan

International Thomson Publishing GmbH
Königswinterer Strasse 418
53227 Bonn, Germany

International Thomson Publishing
Southern Africa
Building 18, Constantia Park
240 Old Pretoria Road
Halfway House, 1685 South Africa

ISBN 0-534-53317-5

# STUDY GUIDE
## CONTENTS

# PREFACE

Although humans are fundamentally similar, we have created a wonderful diversity of cultures. Introductory cultural anthropology may be your first approach to the study of distinctive economies, kinship systems, linguistic forms, and political systems as well as many others of the discipline's areas of research. Like other introductory social science and humanities courses, anthropology will help you understand the people with whom you live and work. Anthropology also provides some basics for understanding why people around the world are as different as they are alike. Anthropologists stress the significance of culture, as compared to biology, in the study of human capability.

Many of you will not major in anthropology but will have an opportunity to study a discipline that provides an excellent preparation for any type of work with people, whether in the business world, the international community, or in your own home. The study of anthropology will teach you that our differences have been important for our survival as a species and remain important as we struggle to learn how to care for the earth and its population in the future.

Ferraro's textbooks emphasizes how anthropological knowledge can be applied outside of the classroom. Some of the most valuable lessons from the course are ones you should be able to use after you have finished college. Studying anthropology will challenge and perhaps change your view of the world. It will enable you to better understand the people and institutions you encounter.

The learning objectives at the beginning of each chapter can help you understand what to expect from your reading. If you still have a question about an objective after having completed the work in this study guide, you will know that you need to consult your text again. Of course, you may want to discuss the material with your instructor and fellow students. The purpose of a text, like that of a class, is to help you understand a topic. The purpose of this student guide is to further assist your comprehension of the course material.

The terms introduced in this course are essential for an understanding of anthropology. Even if you are not required to write term papers or keep a journal, you will learn a great deal of anthropology if you make use of the sections of this study guide that involve writing exercises.

The other questions in this guide will assist in your review of the text material. They should reinforce what you have learned in your reading and in the classroom. Most of the fill-in-the-blank questions are from the textbook. You may first answer the questions on separate paper so that you can use this guide again while reviewing for a test. The answers to all of the questions are at the end of the guide.

# CHAPTER
# 1
## WHAT IS ANTHROPOLOGY?

## LEARNING OBJECTIVES

Complete the work in this chapter of the Study Guide to improve your understanding of the following objectives. Read them before you begin and after you have finished the definitions and questions. Write a note to yourself about any objective that is still not clear, reread your text's discussion of that topic, and if you continue to have questions, discuss the issue with your classmates and instructor.

Having read and studied Chapter 1, you should be able to:

1. Comprehend the breadth of the study of anthropology; understand especially its interest in global diversity.

2. Describe the four field approach to anthropology.

3. Understand that the four fields are interrelated and have blurred boundaries.

4. Identify four broad areas of interest to physical anthropologists.

5. Understand why archaeologists analyze material remains of historic and prehistoric cultures.

6. Describe the three types of material remains of interest to archaeologists.

7. Describe the four branches of linguistic anthropology.

8.    Explain the difference between ethnography and ethnology.

9.    Identify five areas of specialization within cultural anthropology.

10.   Understand what holism means in anthropology.

11.   List four contributions of the holistic, cross-cultural perspective of anthropology to the scientific understanding of humanity.

12.   Understand the difference between basic and applied research in anthropology.

## DEFINITIONS AND EXAMPLES

Write out your own definitions and examples from memory.  Compare your answers with those in the book's glossary after defining all of the terms.

Define

1.    anthropology

_____

_____

_____

2.    archaeology

_____

_____

_____

3.    physical anthropology

_____

_____

_____

4.    anthropological linguistics

_____

_____

_____

5.    cultural anthropology

_____

_____

_____

6.    descriptive linguistic

_____

_____

_____

_____

7.    epidemiology

_____

_____

_____

_____

8.    ethnolinguistics

_____

_____

_____

_____

9.    ethnology

_____

_____

_____

_____

10.    genetics

_____

_____

_____

11.    historical linguistics

_____

_____

_____

_____

12.    holism

_____

_____

_____

_____

13.    human paleoanthropology

_____

_____

_____

_____

14.    population biology

_____

_____

_____

_____

15.    primatology

_____

_____

_____

_____

16.    race

_____

_____

_____

_____

17.    sociolinguistics

_____

_____

_____

_____

18.    artifacts

_____

_____

_____

_____

19.    ecofacts

_____

_____

_____

_____

20.     features

_____
_____
_____
_____

21.     glottochronology

_____
_____
_____

22.     paleoanthropology

_____
_____
_____
_____

23.     protohuman

_____
_____
_____
_____

Give an example as well as a definition for the following:

24.     ethnography

_____
_____
_____

**MULTIPLE-CHOICE**

1.    The primates, because they are our nearest living relatives, are studied by

    a.    physical anthropologists.
    b.    archaeologists.
    c.    nonvertebrate paleontologists.
    d.    none of the above

2.    The role of disease in human evolution, nutrition, growth and development are of most interest to

    a.    a medical anthropologist.
    b.    an economic anthropologist.
    c.    an educational anthropologist.
    d.    b and c

3.    Anthropologists may study

    a.    rural to urban migration.
    b.    second language acquisition and use in the home.
    c.    how children learn what they need to know at different stages of development.
    d.    all of the above

4.    The anthropological study of human variation

    a.    only pertains to visible physical traits.
    b.    involves less visible biochemical factors as well as visible physical traits that can influence human survival.
    c.    leaves to biologists the study of human adaptation to the environment.
    d.    only pertains to the biochemical factors that influence human survival.

5.    A linguistic anthropologist studying sound systems, grammatical systems, and the meanings attached to words in specific languages specializes in

    a.    ethnolinguistics.
    b.    descriptive linguistics.
    c.    historical linguistics.
    d.    sociolinguistics.

6.    Studying how linguistic categories can affect how people categorize their experiences, how they think, and how they perceive the world around them is the work of

    a.    historical archaeologists.
    b.    linguistic anthropologists.
    c.    physical anthropologists.
    d.    prehistoric archaeologists.

7.    A difference among artifacts, features, and ecofacts is that

    a.    artifacts and features are made by humans.
    b.    features and ecofacts can not be taken from the environment for study in the laboratory.
    c.    arrowheads are artifacts, post holes are features, and seeds are ecofacts.
    d.    all of the above

8.    An example of an ethnography is

    a.    a description of the culture of a group of people from the South American highlands who have migrated to the rain forest.
    b.    a report on the archaeological sites of the first African state societies.
    c.    a study of a South American indigenous language.
    d.    all of the above

9.    Holism in anthropology involves a consideration of both the biological and cultural aspects of human behavior and

    a.    human diversity in the twentieth century.
    b.    only human societies of the last two centuries.
    c.    human evolution and culture over the last several million years.
    d.    human evolution and culture over the last three billion years.

10.    The best subjects for anthropological research are found in

    a.    industrialized societies.
    b.    prehistoric societies.
    c.    peasant societies.
    d.    all of the above

11.    Holism in anthropology is demonstrated in

   a.    a narrow focus on contemporary societies.
   b.    an emphasis on the important of the sociocultural environment without a recognition of genetics contributions to humanity.
   c.    its study of many different aspects of human experience.
   d.    an emphasis on the important of genetics without a recognition of the sociocultural environment's contributions to humanity.

12.    Economic anthropologists study how

   a.    goods and services are produced.
   b.    goods and services are distributed.
   c.    goods and services are consumed.
   d.    all of the above

13.    Learning about anthropology will increase your knowledge of exotic cultures, but perhaps even more importantly it will

   a.    teach you about the origins of Western values.
   b.    help you understand your own culture.
   c.    teach you how superior non-industrialized societies are.
   d.    all of the above

14.    Anthropology is concerned primarily with the scientific study of culture and

   a.    properly focuses on exotic cultures.
   b.    properly focuses on the contribution of historical societies to contemporary human cultures.
   c.    because our lives and our jobs are conducted within a cultural context, anthropologists have done research which has practical relevance to our everyday lives.
   d.    has limited practical relevance to our everyday lives because of its focus on excavating past societies material remains.

15.    The term anthropology means the study of humans and

   a.    the broadest of all the disciplines that study humans.
   b.    it strives to understand the biological origins of humans.
   c.    it strives to understand the behavior and thoughts of humans.
   d.    all of the above

**TRUE-FALSE**

_____ 1.     Stone tools are more likely to be studied by anthropologists than are marriage customs or street gangs.

_____ 2.     Anthropology is the broadest in scope of all the disciplines that study humans and is interested in global diversity.

_____ 3.     Anthropologists attempt to understand the human condition and span the gap between the humanities, the social sciences, and the natural sciences.

_____ 4.     Primate behavior is of interest to anthropologists because primates are our closest non-human relatives.

_____ 5.     Anthropologists have studied the health and nutrition of a medieval Nubian population in the Sudan.

_____ 6.     The study of anthropology looks at the human condition from a contemporary perspective not from an evolutionary one.

_____ 7.     Archaeologists study a short period of prehistory and a very long historic period.

_____ 8.     Artifacts and ecofacts are made by humans.

_____ 9.     Basic and applied research have very different goals.

_____ 10.     Today few cultural anthropologists do research in the United States or seek employment outside of universities.

_____ 11.     The comparative perspective of anthropology helps us to better understand ourselves and others.

_____ 12.     The concepts of reason, logic, and rationality had their sole origin in ancient Greece.

_____ 13.     Educational anthropologists work only in Third World nations.

_____ 14.     Applied anthropology gains scientific understanding for its own sake.

_____ 15.     Linguistic anthropologists may study how English is used in a modern American classroom.

_____ 16.    Psychological anthropology looks at the relationship between culture and the psychological makeup of individuals and groups.

_____ 17.    Archaeologists look at the material remains of past societies in order to learn more about their ways of life.

_____ 18.    Applied research in anthropology has little impact on our personal and professional lives.

_____ 19.    Clifford Geertz has said that one of the tasks of anthropology is to unsettle, "to keep the world off balance."

_____ 20.    There are fewer applied anthropologists today than there were three decades ago.

## MATCHING

Match the following sub-fields with the type of research done by anthropologists working within them.

a.    archaeology
b.    linguistic anthropology
c.    cultural anthropology
d.    physical anthropology

1.    _____    studying the exchange of needles by heroin addicts
2.    _____    studying tribal political roles
3.    _____    studying the impact of a new road on a small community
4.    _____    studying chimpanzees and gorillas
5.    _____    studying the relationship between social class and language usage
6.    _____    studying how to design buildings for a Native American school
7.    _____    studying the evolution of human locomotion
8.    _____    studying the language skills of a group being sued by a governmental agency
9.    _____    studying alcohol use among young people in an urban community
10.   _____    studying the kinship system of Greek peasants
11.   _____    excavating a prehistoric settlement site
12.   _____    studying a tribe's terms for colors of cattle
13.   _____    studying stone tools
14.   _____    studying the hunting knowledge of an Eskimo group
15.   _____    studying a South American system of agriculture

Determine which of the following types of research are applied or basic anthropology.

a.    applied anthropology
b.    basic anthropology

16. _____    studying the exchange of needles by heroin addicts
17. _____    studying tribal political roles
18. _____    studying the impact of a new road on a small community
19. _____    studying chimpanzees and gorillas
20. _____    studying the relationship between social class and language usage
21. _____    studying how to design buildings for a Native American school
22. _____    studying the evolution of human locomotion
23. _____    studying the language skills of a group being sued by a governmental agency
24. _____    studying alcohol use among young people in an urban community
25. _____    studying the kinship system of Greek peasants
26. _____    excavating a prehistoric settlement site
27. _____    studying a tribe's terms for colors of cattle
28. _____    studying stone tools
29. _____    studying the hunting knowledge of an Eskimo group
30. _____    studying a South American system of agriculture

## SHORT ANSWER

1.    What does the term anthropology mean?  How is it different from other social sciences?

2.    What do we learn from comparing aspects of culture across societies?  Why is cross-cultural comparison important?

3.    What is the difference between applied and basic research?

4.      What are the sub-fields of anthropology?

5.      Why is it important for anthropology to examine all aspects of humanity for all periods of time and for all parts of the globe?

# CHAPTER
## 2
## THE CONCEPT OF CULTURE

**LEARNING OBJECTIVES**

Complete the work in this chapter of the Study Guide to improve your understanding of the following objectives. Read them before you begin and after you have finished the definitions and questions. Write a note to yourself about any objective that is still not clear, reread your text's discussion of that topic, and if you continue to have questions, discuss the issue with your classmates and instructor.

Having read and studied Chapter 2, you should be able to:

1.  Give a clear definition of the anthropological concept of culture and recognize what is included in this concept.

2.  Explain the significance of the shared nature of culture.

3.  Define culture shock and explain when it is likely to be experienced.

4.  State four reasons why different members of a society have distinct understandings of their culture.

5.  Explain the importance of learning for culture acquisition and the lesser significance of instinctive behavior for humans.

6.    Give several examples of how humans do things because of what they have learned from their culture.

7.    Explain how culture can affect our physical bodies and biological processes.

8.    Understand that cultures are constantly changing and give examples of cultural innovation and diffusion.

9.    Understand the nature and limitations of ethnocentric reactions and give several examples of their own and others' ethnocentrism.

10.    Present a clear explanation of cultural relativism and its importance to anthropology.

11.    Understand why anthropologists are interested in the similarities as well as the differences among human cultures.

12.    Understand what cultural universals are and be able to give several examples of such universals.

13.    Describe how, for all human societies, culture is an important form of adaptation to environment.

14.    Explain what it means to say culture is integrated and what that implies about the process of culture change.

## DEFINITIONS AND EXAMPLES

Write out your own definitions and examples from memory.  Compare your answers with those in the book's glossary after defining all of the terms.

Define

1.    adaptive nature of culture

_____
_____
_____
_____

2.    organic analogy

_____
_____
_____
_____

3.     tableau raise

_____
_____
_____
_____

Give an example as well as a definition for the following:

4.     cultural diffusion

_____
_____
_____
_____

5.     cultural relativism

_____
_____
_____
_____

6.     cultural universal

_____
_____
_____
_____

7.     enculturation

_____
_____
_____
_____

8.     ethnocentrism

_____
_____
_____
_____

9.     innovation

_____
_____
_____
_____

10.    basic needs

_____
_____
_____
_____

11.    culture shock

_____
_____
_____
_____

## MULTIPLE-CHOICE

1.    The anthropological concept of culture includes

    a.    instinctual behavior of individuals.
    b.    all human thought.
    c.    ideas and learned ways of behaving.
    d.    the way humans reproduce.

2.    People experience culture shock when they are

    a.    around people with shared ideas and a language that are different than theirs.
    b.    exposed to a culture they don't understand.
    c.    in a society when people have learned to behave in ways different than their own.
    d.    all of the above

3.    Cultural relativism is

    a.    a type of extreme nationalism.
    b.    a type of prejudice.
    c.    judging a culture by its own context and not though comparison with your own.
    d.    a and b

4.    Learning is an important influence on

    a.    our ways of thinking.
    b.    our ways of behaving.
    c.    the material goods we make and use.
    d.    all of the above

5.    People acquire their culture

   a.    most efficiently in Europe.
   b.    most efficiently in Africa, Latin America, and Asia.
   c.    in very different way in each society of the world.
   d.    in essentially the same way throughout the world.

6.    Culture determines that people

   a.    have to sleep.
   b.    eat rice with chopsticks.
   c.    must care for children.
   d.    need protection from extremes of temperature.

7.    When people in a society do not behave or think in the same way

   a.    their behavior is concrete proof that their society is disintegrating.
   b.    their society cannot continue to exist much longer.
   c.    it may be because of differences in social class or personal history.
   d.    a and b

8.    Ideas about beauty and the preferred shape of the human form

   a.    are cultural.
   b.    vary from society to society.
   c.    vary little from one society to another.
   d.    a and b

9.    Human's heavy reliance on cultural learning for their survival is important because

   a.    it means that behavior can change and more adaptive ideas and ways of doing
         things can be learned.
   b.    industrialized nations always have the most adaptive cultures and therefore the
         most to teach other societies.
   c.    industrialized nations have little to learn from other societies.
   d.    a and c

10.    People in some societies have bound feet, use scarification, or apply body paint because they

    a.    believe these practices beautify their bodies.
    b.    don't understand that they are harming their body.
    c.    don't understand basic biology.
    d.    they have no concept of beauty and health.

11.    A strong negative reaction to an unfamiliar religion is an example of

    a.    diffusion.
    b.    ethnocentrism.
    c.    cultural relativism.
    d.    enculturation.

12.    The organic analogy

    a.    emphasizes the dysfunction of selected aspects of culture.
    b.    emphasizes the function of aspects of human culture.
    c.    means that human culture is systemic in a way similar to the systems that function together to maintain a living body.
    d.    b and c

13.    Although indigenous to South America, potatoes are important in the diets of many societies around the world; this is an example of

    a.    cultural diffusion.
    b.    cultural relativism.
    c.    a cultural universal.
    d.    an independent invention.

14.    It is difficult to plan cultural change because

    a.    culture is integrated.
    b.    people always resist any aspect of culture introduced from outside.
    c.    although technology changes, people's ideas do not.
    d.    although people's ideas change, technology does not.

15.    "Small-scale" describes a society that

    a.    has a relatively small population.
    b.    is technologically simple.
    c.    has little labor specialization.
    d.    a and b
    e.    all of the above

16.    Enculturation means

    a.    learning culture from other members of your own society.
    b.    going into a different culture.
    c.    transporting culture from one society to another.
    d.    improving the culture of another society.

17.    Esber's research as a cultural advisor to the Payson Project

    a.    used a variety of research methods to gather information on Apache use of space in houses.
    b.    caused the U.S. government to terminate its project on providing housing for the Apache.
    c.    demonstrates the suitability of Anglo housing for the Apache on the reservation.
    d.    a and b

18.    Humans have culture

    a.    because it is genetic.
    b.    because it is always formally taught within a nuclear family's household.
    c.    only because it is formally taught in public school.
    d.    because it is learned in every societies around the world.

19.    Nineteenth century anthropology

    a.    excluded all racists.
    b.    included people who were ethnocentric.
    c.    used only objective language, unlike other disciplines at that time.
    d.    a and c

20.    While all humans have culture,

    a.    deviance from cultural norms is found in all societies.
    b.    all people have the option of doing some things differently from what is culturally expected.
    c.    most individuals operate almost independently of their society's norms.
    d.    a and b

**TRUE-FALSE**

_____ 1.    Culture includes our shared behavioral patterns but not thoughts .

_____ 2.    Anthropologists argue that all humans have culture, not just those who like opera and ballet.

_____ 3.    Cultural relativism requires that we view all cultures as morally equivalent.

_____ 4.    A very small part of our behavioral responses is the result of complex learning processes.

_____ 5.    People's values, ideas, attitudes, and material possessions are part of culture.

_____ 6.    No other animal has a greater capacity for learning than do humans.

_____ 7.    Even in radically different cultures, children share the experience of having to learn shared ways of thinking and acting.

_____ 8.    Anthropologists today emphasize the importance of instincts rather than the notion of tabula rasa.

_____ 9.    No nation has a monopoly on ethnocentrism.

_____ 10.    The biological process of human digestion can be influenced by culture.

_____ 11.    Small-scale, nonwestern societies experience very rapid culture change more frequently than large-scale, western societies.

_____ 12.    Cultural diffusion is the invention of new ways of thinking or behaving.

_____ 13.    Every aspect of culture is either adaptive or maladaptive.

_____ 14.    Ethnocentrism is a non-biased way of viewing the world through the lens of one's own culture.

_____ 15.    Most cultural elements found in any society are the result of invention.

_____ 16.    Cultural relativism is a methodology not an ethical stance.

_____ 17.    Innovation is the ultimate source of all culture change.

_____ 18.    Economic systems, although they vary in detail, are cultural universals.

_____ 19.    Culture is the reason humans can survive in such a wide variety of natural environments.

_____ 20.    Cultural universals are common features shared by all cultures of the world.

_____ 21.    Becoming aware of our ethnocentrism allows us to eliminate it totally.

_____ 22.    Skyscrapers, computers, and creation myths are not part of culture.

_____ 23.    Cultural relativists attempt to understand how a cultural item fits into the rest of the cultural system rather than comparing other cultures with their own.

_____ 24.    Cultures change because of external mechanisms not internal ones.

_____ 25.    Some cultural practices, such as genocide, are morally indefensible within any cultural context.

## SHORT ANSWER

1.    What are the two basic processes of cultural change within a society?

2.    What is ethnocentrism and why is it important in anthropology and in life?

3.    What is the importance of cultural adaptation for human existence cross-culturally?

4.     What is holism in anthropology?


5.     Why is the word "primitive" ethnocentric?


6.     Give two examples of ethnocentrism and explain how it is harmful?

# CHAPTER
## 3
## APPLIED ANTHROPOLOGY

## LEARNING OBJECTIVES

Complete the work in this chapter of the Study Guide to improve your understanding of the following objectives. Read them before you begin and after you have finished the definitions and questions. Write a note to yourself about any objective that is still not clear, reread your text's discussion of that topic, and if you continue to have questions, discuss the issue with your classmates and instructor.

Having read and studied Chapter 3, you should be able to:

1.  Distinguish between applied and pure anthropology while recognizing their mutually supportive relationship.

2.  Understand that most applied research is conducted under the sponsorship of international, national, and private organizations rather than in an academic setting.

3.  Describe the variety of specialized roles through which applied anthropologists work.

4.  Discuss the significance of participant-observation, holistic perspective, regional expertise, emic view, and cultural relativism as they pertain to applied anthropology.

5.  Summarize the major social and historical factors influencing the development of applied anthropology from the 1930's to the present.

6.    Describe the major ethical issues involved in Project Camelot and the consequences affecting legitimate anthropological research.

7.    Clearly distinguish among the following areas of responsibility for anthropologists: to their subjects, to their profession, to their colleagues, and to their own professional goals.

8.    Understand the ethical issues involved in applied work and summarize the Statement on Ethics of the American Anthropological Association.


## DEFINITIONS AND EXAMPLES

Write out your own definitions and examples from memory.  Compare your answers with those in the book's glossary after defining all of the terms.

Define

1.    cultural relativism

_____
_____
_____


2.    emic view

_____
_____
_____


3.    etic view

_____
_____
_____


4.    evaluator

_____
_____
_____


5.    Fox Project

_____
_____
_____

6.    new applied anthropology

_____

_____

_____

7.    participant-observation

_____

_____

_____

8.    Project Camelot

_____

_____

_____

9.    Vicos Project

_____

_____

_____

10.   value-free philosophy

_____

_____

_____

11.   advocate

_____

_____

_____

12.   research analyst

_____

_____

_____

13.   cultural broker

_____

_____

_____

14.    expert witness

_____
_____
_____

15.    impact assessor

_____
_____
_____

16.    needs assessor

_____
_____
_____

17.    planner

_____
_____
_____

18.    trainer

_____
_____
_____

19.    administrator/manager

_____
_____
_____

20.    policy researcher

_____
_____
_____

Give an example as well as a definition for the following:

21.    holistic perspective

_____
_____
_____

22.    regional expertise

_____

_____

_____

## MULTIPLE-CHOICE

1.    The emic view is held by

    a.    government officials.
    b.    academics.
    c.    local clients of applied anthropologists.
    d.    a and b

2.    Anthropology aimed very explicitly at practical results is referred to as

    a.    modernization anthropology.
    b.    applied anthropology.
    c.    physical anthropology.
    d.    new age anthropology.

3.    Because of an early association with colonialism, applied anthropology traditionally had

    a.    a relatively negative image due to close contact with administrators rather than indigenous people.
    b.    a history of being less serious than other types of anthropology.
    c.    an image of being old fashioned.
    d.    none of the above.

4.    Applied anthropological research is often used by

    a.    U. S. Agency for International Development.
    b.    private corporations.
    c.    U.S. Department of Agriculture.
    d.    all of the above

5.    Applied anthropology

    a.    has little relevance for problems in industrialized societies.
    b.    is characterized by theoretical-oriented research among the world's contemporary populations.
    c.    is characterized by problem-oriented research among the world's contemporary populations.
    d.    has little relevance for problems of contemporary non-industrialized societies.

6.    An applied anthropologist who imparts cultural knowledge about certain populations to different groups that are expected to work in cross-cultural situations:  this is essentially a teaching role.

    a.    advocate
    b.    trainer
    c.    expert witness
    d.    administrator/manager

7.    In the past some anthropologists considered applied anthropology

    a.    a provider of service but not a legitimate area of research.
    b.    the most prestigious field within the discipline.
    c.    the branch of the discipline which works to help non-industrialized societies prevent change from occurring in their cultures.
    d.    a and c

8.    Anthropology contributes to the understanding of sociocultural realities through its

    a.    participant-observation methodology.
    b.    holistic perspective
    c.    emic view.
    d.    a and b
    e.    all of the above

9.    Local clients in applied research have

    a.    an etic view.
    b.    little understanding of their own needs.
    c.    almost no technical knowledge.
    d.    an emic view.

10.     Applied anthropologists, like other cultural anthropologists, have

    a.     a narrow specialization in the discipline.
    b.     little cultural relativism.
    c.     a better understanding of bureaucrats than of indigenous people.
    d.     a long-term association with a cultural region.

11.     The amount of time required for most applied anthropological research is

    a.     about twice as long as that for pure anthropological research.
    b.     usually much shorter than that required for pure anthropological research.
    c.     always decided by the researcher.
    d.     always decided by the agency or company hiring the anthropologist.

12.     Contributions by anthropologists to the war effort during World War II

    a.     helped the federal government make important decisions on the conduct of relations with our allies as well as our adversaries.
    b.     was always very open and non-controversial.
    c.     met all of the ethical standards of today.
    d.     all of the above

13.     Applied anthropology in the 1990s is

    a.     limited to research in cultural anthropology.
    b.     primarily forensic anthropology.
    c.     a distinct subfield of the discipline.
    d.     difficult to define because it has always been a part of the discipline and cuts across all four traditional subfields.

14.     Pure anthropologists

    a.     have some concern for the practical implications of their research.
    b.     have no concern for the practical implications of their research.
    c.     are indebted to applied anthropologists for stimulating interest in new areas of research.
    d.     a and c

15.    The Cornell-Peru Vicos Project

    a.    involved only anthropologists from Cornell University in the work in Peru.
    b.    involved Cornell and Peruvian anthropologists working together in Vicos.
    c.    was unsuccessful in empowering farmers in Vicos, Peru.
    d.    was a valiant but unsuccessful attempt to support farmers who tried to purchase the land they had been working.

16.    The value systems of applied anthropologists

    a.    may be very different from those of the populations with whom they work.
    b.    seldom conflict with the values of the populations with whom they work.
    c.    should be made explicit to their clients.
    d.    a and c
    e.    a and b

17.    The ethical conduct of anthropologists is determined

    a.    by their national association, the American Anthropological Association.
    b.    solely by their nation's laws.
    c.    ultimately by their own values.
    d.    by their international association, the World Anthropological Association.

18.    Project Camelot was

    a.    strongly criticized for allegedly involving questionable ethical behavior.
    b.    conducted with funding from the U.S. Army.
    c.    designed to gather data on counterinsurgency that would enable the U.S. Army to cope more effectively with internal revolutions in foreign countries.
    d.    all of the above

19.    Approximately what percent of all anthropology Ph. D.s work outside an academic setting for government organizations, nonprofits, or private-sector firms?

    a.    90%
    b.    30%
    c.    50%
    d.    70%

20.    Anthropologists working on the island of Truk

    a.    gathered information from the local people and from the government.
    b.    were asked to leave because the local people found out they were government agents working for the establishment of an airport.
    c.    never developed fluency in the local language and therefore gained more knowledge about the government's position than that of the local populations.
    d.    prevented the building of an airport because of their own ethics and political views.

21.    It is a common role for applied anthropologists, involving the use of research skills to determine how well a program or policy has succeeded in its objectives.

    a.    evaluator
    b.    planner
    c.    trainer
    d.    impact assessor

22.    Measures the effect of a particular project, program, or policy on local people:  may determine the consequences, both intended and unintended.

    a.    impact assessor
    b.    planner
    c.    trainer
    d.    evaluator

23.    Anthropologists finance their research through grants from sponsors and must

    a.    consider the purposes of their sponsoring organizations and the possible uses any agency might have for their findings.
    b.    always reveal sources of information to their sponsors.
    c.    never accept a salary from a supporting agency.
    d.    accept all ethical decisions made by any sponsor.

24.    Research on Gypsy culture suggests that when working with them as patients,

    a.    older relatives should be kept separate from younger patients.
    b.    they are always impressed with the cleanliness of hospitals.
    c.    they should not be separated from family and friends.
    d.    that it is important to talk to them as if they had no difficulties with English no matter what their language skills are.

**TRUE-FALSE**

_____ 1.    Anthropologists have a responsibility to their subjects, their discipline, and their colleagues.

_____ 2.    Archaeologists had to develop new methods and theories in order to study contemporary landfills and help develop policies on solid waste disposal.

_____ 3.    It is only since the 1960's that anthropologists have become concerned with the utility of their findings for solving social problems.

_____ 4.    Pure rather than applied anthropologists look at research problems in terms of both short term and long term results.

_____ 5.    During World War II applied anthropologists worked on national character studies.

_____ 6.    Anthropologists were never hired by colonial governments to conduct research on native populations until the decades after World War II.

_____ 7.    Anthropologists have always used more quantitative than qualitative methods.

_____ 8.    The emic view is the perspective of the bureaucrats of the country where applied anthropological research is conducted.

_____ 9.    Some anthropologists argue that applied research compromises cultural relativity.

_____ 10.    No individual anthropologists practice both applied and pure anthropology.

_____ 11.    Applied anthropologists work only outside the United States.

_____ 12.    A common role for applied anthropologists is that of the advocate which involves political action in active support of a particular group of people.

_____ 13.    National and local associations are playing a growing role in the training and professional lives of applied anthropologists.

_____ 14.    For applied anthropologists, ethical issues are complex because their research brings them into contact with people who have different and conflicting value systems.

_____ 15.    The holistic perspective forces anthropologists to look at multiple variables and see human problems in their historical, economic, and cultural context.

_____ 16.    Very few anthropologists today are culture area specialists who focus on an ethnographic region.

_____ 17.    Only the Society for Applied Anthropology has identified areas of ethical responsibility for practicing anthropologists.

_____ 18.    The Vicos Project was an example of anthropological intervention with a Native American group in Iowa and the code name, the Fox Project, refers to a project in Peru, South America.

_____ 19.    A value-free philosophy refers to a methodology which allows anthropological research to ignore the values of the individuals studied and those of the anthropologists.

_____ 20.    One very important ethical issue to which applied anthropologists must be sensitive is whether or not the people being studied will benefit from the changes proposed by a development project.

## MATCHING

Match the following.

a.    policy researcher
b.    evaluator
c.    impact assessor
d.    planner
e.    research analyst
f.    needs assessor
g.    trainer
h.    advocate
i.    expert witness
j.    administrator/manager
k.    cultural broker

1. _____    imparts cultural knowledge about certain populations to different groups that are expected to work in cross-cultural situations.
2. _____    actively participates in the design of various programs, policies, and projects.
3. _____    uses research skills to determine how well a program or policy has succeeded in its objectives
4. _____    an active supporter of a particular group of people; usually involves some political action
5. _____    serves as a liaison between the program planner and/or administrators and the local ethnic communities
6. _____    provides cultural data to policy makers so they can make the most informed policy decisions
7. _____    interprets research findings so that policy makers, planners, and administrators can make more culturally sensitive decisions
8. _____    presents culturally relevant research findings as part of judicial proceedings through legal briefs, depositions, or direct testimony
9. _____    measures the effect that a particular project, program or policy has on local people
10. _____    conducts research to determine ahead of time the need for a proposed program or project
11. _____    assumes direct administrative responsibility for a particular project

## SHORT ANSWER

1.    What are the differences between pure and applied anthropology?

2.    Why do anthropologists participate in attempts to change cultures in applied projects?

3.    In what types of setting do applied anthropologists work?

4.    What is the contribution of participant-observation and the holistic perspective to applied anthropology?

5.    What determines the ethics of applied research?

6.    To what communities and groups do applied anthropologists have ethical responsibilities?

# CHAPTER
# 4
# THE GROWTH OF ANTHROPOLOGICAL THEORY

## LEARNING OBJECTIVES

Complete the work in this chapter of the Study Guide to improve your understanding of the following objectives. Read them before you begin and after you have finished the definitions and questions. Write a note to yourself about any objective that is still not clear, reread your text's discussion of that topic, and if you continue to have questions, discuss the issue with your classmates and instructor.

Having read and studied Chapter 4, you should be able to:

1.    Give a precise definition of theory and explain what issues anthropological theories attempt to address.

2.    Describe the cultural evolutionary theory of Tylor and Morgan, and recognize its limitations and the significance of their distinction between cultural and biological processes.

3.    Recognize the limitations of both the British and the German diffusion theories and the importance of the questions why do some traits arise in the first place and why do certain ones spread throughout a geographical region while others do not.

4.    Understand the significance of Boas' emphasis on the importance of history and ethnographic fieldwork, his contribution to methodological rigor, and his stance against racism and genetic determinism.

5.    Describe functionalist theory and distinguish between Malinowski's and Radcliffe-Brown's approaches to the meaning of function.

6.    Comprehend the concepts of universal functions, functional unity, and Merton's criticisms of those concepts.

7.    Summarize psychological anthropologists' positions on the connection between personality, the individual, and culture; and recognize the theoretical contributions of Sapir, Benedict, and Margaret Mead.

8.    Distinguish between the neoevolutionary theories of Leslie White and Julian Steward.

9.    Understand the meaning of structure for French structuralist theory, the contributions of Levi-Strauss to that theory, and the importance it gives to the structure of the human mind.

10.    Recognize the importance of the linguistic model and the emic view for ethnoscience.

11.    Explain the focus of cultural materialism, the significance of etic research methodology for it, and why it is not a Marxist theory.

12.    Discuss the importance of self-knowledge, ideas, and values for interpretive anthropology and its humanistic approach.

13.    Understand how to use HRAF data for statistical cross-cultural comparison and the limitation of such data.

## DEFINITIONS AND EXAMPLES

Write out your own definitions and examples from memory.  Compare your answers with those in the book's glossary after defining all of the terms.

Define

1.    theory

_____

_____

_____

2.    diffusionism

_____

_____

_____

3.    ethnoscience

_____

_____

_____


4.    evolutionism

_____

_____

_____


5.    French structuralism

_____

_____

_____


6.    functionalism

_____

_____

_____


7.    multilinear evolution

_____

_____

_____


8.    neoevolution

_____

_____

_____


9.    structural functionalism

_____

_____

_____


10.   unilinear evolutionism

_____

_____

_____

11.   universal evolution

_____
_____
_____

12.   barbarism

_____
_____
_____

13.   civilization

_____
_____
_____

14.   dysfunction

_____
_____
_____

15.   functional unity

_____
_____
_____

16.   kulturkreise

_____
_____
_____

17.   mother-in-law avoidance

_____
_____
_____

18.   psychic unity

_____
_____
_____

19.    psychological anthropology

_____
_____
_____

20.    savagery

_____
_____
_____

21.    universal functions

_____
_____
_____

22.    Human Relations Area Files (HRAF)

_____
_____
_____

23.    cultural materialism

_____
_____
_____

24.    interpretive anthropology

_____
_____
_____

25.    cultural ecology

_____
_____
_____

26.    deductive

_____
_____
_____

27.    hypothesis

_____
_____
_____

28.    inductive

_____
_____
_____

29.    latent function

_____
_____
_____

30.    manifest function

_____
_____
_____

31.    synchronic approach

_____
_____
_____

Identify the theory associated with each of the following persons and its place in history.

32.    Ruth Benedict

_____
_____
_____

33.    Franz Boas

_____
_____
_____

34.    Clifford Geertz

_____
_____
_____

35.   Fritz Graebner

_____

_____

_____

36.   Marvin Harris

_____

_____

_____

37.   Claude Levi-Strauss

_____

_____

_____

38.   Bronislav Malinowski

_____

_____

_____

39.   Margaret Mead

_____

_____

_____

40.   Louis Henry Morgan

_____

_____

_____

41.   George Peter Murdock

_____

_____

_____

42.   W. J. Perry

_____

_____

_____

43.    A.R. Radcliffe-Brown

_____
_____
_____

44.    Edward Sapir

_____
_____
_____

45.    Wilhelm Schmidt

_____
_____
_____

46.    Grafton Elliot Smith

_____
_____
_____

47.    Julian Steward

_____
_____
_____

48.    Edward Tylor

_____
_____
_____

49.    Leslie White

_____
_____
_____

## MULTIPLE-CHOICE

1.    A theory

    a.    reduces reality into an abstract set of principles.
    b.    suggests a relationship between phenomena.
    c.    explains and predicts.
    d.    all of the above

2.    Which of the following was one of the stages in nineteenth century evolutionary theory?

    a.    barbarism
    b.    primitive
    c.    modern
    d.    traditional

3.    Which theory first included a cultural interpretation of human differences?

    a.    multilineal theory
    b.    structural theory
    c.    functional theory
    d.    evolutionary theory

4.    What theory emphasized the need for explanations of contact between cultures?

    a.    neoevolutionary theory
    b.    structural theory
    c.    diffusion theory
    d.    functionalist theory

5.    The American historicism approach was developed by

    a.    Louis Henry Morgan.
    b.    Alfred Radcliffe-Brown.
    c.    Claude Levi-Strauss.
    d.    Franz Boas.

6.    The functionalist theory which focused on how cultures meet the needs of individuals was developed by

    a.    Leslie White.
    b.    George Steward.
    c.    Bronislav Malinowski.
    d.    Louis Henry Morgan.

7.    Which anthropologist argued that it was premature to theorize on a small and unreliable database and that anthropology must become more inductive?

    a.    Claude Levi-Strauss
    b.    Alfred Radcliffe-Brown
    c.    Bronislav Malinowski
    d.    Franz Boas

8.    Which theorist argued that while every cultural item *may* have a function, it is wrong to assume they all *must* have a function?

    a.    Robert Merton
    b.    Alfred Radcliffe-Brown
    c.    Bronislav Malinowski
    d.    Franz Boas

9.    Which anthropologist rejected the notion that culture exists above the individual and held that it was in the interaction of individual that was the true center of culture.

    a.    Margaret Mead
    b.    Ruth Benedict
    c.    Edward Sapir
    d.    all of the above

10.    According to Ruth Benedict, cultures

    a.    always include individuals with personalities which are violent, aggressive, and excessive.
    b.    always include individuals with personalities which are restrained, peaceful, and moderate.
    c.    are really individual personalities generalized to the whole culture.
    d.    all of the above

11.    The idea, first found in evolutionary theory, of a sequence of stages

    a.    is the dominant modern theory.
    b.    has been transformed in neoevolutionary theory.
    c.    has been totally discarded in anthropology.
    d.    was part of an argument that it is biological differences that distinguish human populations.

12.    Diffusionism stresses

    a.    the transfer of culture from one society to another.
    b.    how inventive Europeans have been.
    c.    how distinctive every cultures is.
    d.    cultural inventions.

13.    Leslie White and Julian Steward developed the theory of

   a.    evolution.
   b.    structuralism.
   c.    neoevolutionism.
   d.    diffusionism.

14.    Ethnoscience is the approach in which researchers

   a.    infer mental structures or codes from cultural traits.
   b.    infer mental structures or codes from social traits.
   c.    attempt to understand a culture from the point of view of the people themselves.
   d.    attempt to develop a totally logical approach to the study of culture.

15.    The Human Relations Area File

   a.    is only located at Yale University.
   b.    contains only data of extremely high quality.
   c.    contains data that describe a wide range of types of social systems.
   d.    only contains data from definitely independent cases.

16.    Boas and Malinowski both emphasized

   a.    culture sharing.
   b.    cultural diffusion.
   c.    fieldwork.
   d.    brain structure.

17.    For which anthropologist was social and cultural change of great significance?

   a.    Radcliffe-Brown
   b.    Malinowski
   c.    Levi-Strauss
   d.    Julian Steward

18.    The careful collection of empirical data on as many specific cultures as possible was an important focus of work of which theorist?

   a.    Louis Henry Morgan
   b.    Bronislav Malinowski
   c.    Robert Lowie
   d.    Franz Boas

19.    Leslie White focused on

    a.    the adaptation of ideology to environment.
    b.    the harnessing of energy in adapting to the environment.
    c.    the development of laws in small, technologically simple cultures.
    d.    the development of universal functions.

20.    The Trobriand Islands are well known in anthropology because they were the site of a long and uninterrupted period of field work conducted by

    a.    Claude Levi-Strauss.
    b.    Alfred Radcliffe-Brown.
    c.    Bronislav Malinowski.
    d.    Franz Boas.

21.    French structuralism concentrates on

    a.    technological adaptation to the environment.
    b.    identifying mental structures that influence how humans organize socially and culturally.
    c.    the economic organization of societies.
    d.    the political organization of societies.

22.    For Marvin Harris, the significance of ideas and political activities

    a.    is totally ignored.
    b.    is the focus of his theory of cultural materialism because ideas allow humans to make material things.
    c.    is that they can accelerate or retard cultural change.
    d.    all of the above

23.    Clifford Geertz and other interpretive anthropologists seek to explain a single culture by examining

    a.    how the people themselves interpret their own values and behaviors.
    b.    the integration of all aspects of it.
    c.    the functions of the culture in meeting the population's basic needs.
    d.    its history.

24.    Margaret Mead's major contribution to anthropological theory was her demonstration of the importance of

       a.    cultural rather than biological conditioning.
       b.    using quantitative methodologies.
       c.    applied anthropology
       d.    Freudian theory in explaining cross-cultural universals.

25.    Interpretive anthropologists argue that the most important factors in human behavior are

       a.    objective conditions under which people live.
       b.    the way in which the human mind is organized.
       c.    the functions of social, economic, and political life.
       d.    the ways people perceive and classify the conditions under which they live.

**TRUE-FALSE**

_____ 1.    Unproven theories are useful as long as they can generate hypotheses.

_____ 2.    Tylor and Morgan used the notion of function to account for the diversity of human societies.

_____ 3.    A fundamental concept of Levi-Strauss' theory is that human minds think in binary opposition.

_____ 4.    Nineteenth century evolutionists were ethnocentric.

_____ 5.    The Human Relations Area Files (HRAF) is the world's largest anthropological data retrieval system.

_____ 6.    Ethnoscience is not cognitive, unlike French structuralism.

_____ 7.    Leslie White and Julian Steward were interested in continuity in human cultures.

_____ 8.    The relationships between culture and the individual were of interest to Tylor and Radcliffe-Brown.

_____ 9.    Julian Steward did not assume that all cultures passed through the same stages.

_____ 10.    The HRAF has data on all Western and nonwestern societies but research on that data confronts the problem of functional unity.

_____ 11.    The British diffusionists held that all cultural features, wherever they may be found, had their origins in southern Africa.

_____ 12.    Malinowski, a strong advocate of fieldwork, did little such research himself.

_____ 13.    Like the British diffusionists, the German-Austrians focused on particular cultural traits.

_____ 14.    Sapir suggested that individuals learn their cultural patterns unconsciously, unlike their conscious learning of language.

_____ 15.    The early evolutionists developed their theory to establish that human behavior was the result of biological processes.

_____ 16.    Geertz advocates combining self-knowledge with knowledge of the people under study so anthropologists learn something about themselves at the same time they learn about the culture of the informant.

_____ 17.    Merton argued that while all parts of a culture serve a function they are not necessarily connected to one another in functional unity.

_____ 18.    While anthropological theory has changed over time it is still as vital as ever to the design of research.

_____ 19.    Malinowski argued individual needs are more important than the structure and function of society in determining human cultures.

_____ 20.    Margaret Mead's research in Samoa was an exploration of the relationships between culture and the individual.

_____ 21.    Cultural materialists see the prime factors in human behavior as the satisfaction of basic human material needs such as food, water, shelter, and wealth and they rely on etic research.

_____ 22.    Interpretive anthropology relies on etic research and sees anthropology more as a humanistic enterprise than a scientific one.

_____ 23.    Franz Boas' felt the enormous complexity of factors influencing the development of specific cultures rendered any type of sweeping generalization like those of diffusionists and evolutionists inappropriate.

_____ 24.    Interpretive anthropology is relativistic.

_____ 25.     Anthropology theory can help businesspersons be more successful when working outside their own society.

**MATCHING**

Match the following.

a.     Evolutionism
b.     Interpretive Anthropology
c.     HRAF
d.     Structural Functionalism
e.     Psychological Anthropology
f.     Cultural Materialism
g.     French Structuralism
h.     Ethnoscience
i.     American Historical Approach
j.     Neoevolutionism
k.     Functionalist Theory
l.     Diffusionism

1.     _____     Goodenough
2.     _____     Radcliffe-Brown
3.     _____     Benedict
4.     _____     Harris
5.     _____     Mead
6.     _____     Tylor
7.     _____     White
8.     _____     Sapir
9.     _____     Geertz
10.    _____     Sturtevant
11.    _____     Behar
12.    _____     Naroll
13.    _____     Levi-Strauss
14.    _____     Graebner
15.    _____     Boas
16.    _____     Morgan
17.    _____     Smith
18.    _____     Malinowski
19.    _____     Murdock
20.    _____     Perry

## SHORT ANSWER

1.   What is the relationship of theory and hypothesis?  Why is theory important in anthropology?

2.   What were the limitations of unilineal evolutionary and diffusionist theories?

3.   Emic knowledge is important for which anthropological theories?

4.   Etic knowledge is important for which anthropological theories?

5.   How are ethnoscience and interpretive anthropology different?

6.   What is the difference between French structuralist theory, psychological anthropology, and interpretive anthropology?

# CHAPTER
## 5
## METHODS IN CULTURAL ANTHROPOLOGY

## LEARNING OBJECTIVES

Complete the work in this chapter of the Study Guide to improve your understanding of the following objectives. Read them before you begin and after you have finished the definitions and questions. Write a note to yourself about any objective that is still not clear, reread your text's discussion of that topic, and if you continue to have questions, discuss the issue with your classmates and instructor.

Having read and studied Chapter 5, you should be able to:

1.  Discuss the importance of experiential fieldwork to cultural anthropology.

2.  Understand the less romantic aspects of preparing for and carrying out anthropological fieldwork.

3.  Describe the difference between a generalized ethnography and the more focused, problem oriented research usually conducted in recent decades.

4.  Recognize the importance of hypotheses, independent variables, and dependent variables for research design in anthropology.

5.  Discuss the five stages of field research as they were carried out in the Kenya Kinship Study.

6.   Distinguish among the stages of data collection, analysis, and interpretation in field research and recognize the significance each has for the others.

7.   Understand the importance, as well as the limitations, of participant-observation in field work.

8.   Evaluate the appropriate use of both structured and unstructured interviews and be able to suggest ways to determine the validity of the data gathered.

9.   Describe anthropologists' use of mapping, document analysis, genealogies, and photography in fieldwork and recognize that a variety of types of data allows for cross-checking of information.

10.  Understand the nature of culture shock and appreciate the benefits of biculturalism.

11.  Describe how the scientific objectivity of ethnographic fieldwork is different from research in a chemistry or biology laboratory.

12.  Explain what is "narrative ethnography" and why it gives less importance to scientific detachment

## DEFINITIONS AND EXAMPLES

Write out your own definitions and examples from memory.  Compare your answers with those in the book's glossary after defining all of the terms.

Define

1.   analyzing data

   _____
   _____
   _____

2.   census taking

   _____
   _____
   _____

3.   collecting data

   _____
   _____
   _____

4.    culture shock

_____

_____

_____

5.    data analysis

_____

_____

_____

6.    data collection

_____

_____

_____

7.    dependent variable

_____

_____

_____

8.    document analysis

_____

_____

_____

9.    ethnographic mapping

_____

_____

_____

10.    event analysis

_____

_____

_____

11.    fieldwork

_____

_____

_____

12.    genealogy

_____
_____
_____


13.    independent variable

_____
_____
_____


14.    informant

_____
_____
_____


15.    interpreting data

_____
_____
_____


16.    on-farm research

_____
_____
_____


17.    participant-observation

_____
_____
_____


18.    proxemic analysis

_____
_____
_____


19.    research clearance

_____
_____
_____

20.     research design

_____
_____
_____

21.     research proposal

_____
_____
_____

22.     structured interview

_____
_____
_____

23.     unstructured interview

_____
_____
_____


## MULTIPLE-CHOICE

1.      Anthropologists learn about how people in different parts of the world behave and think

   a.      mostly through documentary research.
   b.      by experiential fieldwork.
   c.      primarily from the results of questionnaires.
   d.      primarily from interviewing government and development workers.

2.      Living with the people being studied

   a.      is almost always a part of anthropological fieldwork.
   b.      is part of participant observation.
   c.      helps anthropologists learn about what members of another society know and how they behave.
   d.      all of the above

3.     Fieldwork in another culture is expensive and

    a.     requires anthropologists to spend months writing their proposals for their projects.
    b.     therefore most anthropologists must be independently wealthy.
    c.     getting funding is not as highly competitive as in the 1960s.
    d.     most proposals that are the result of months of hard work are usually funded.
    e.     c and d

4.     Anthropologists may not be able to conduct field research in some countries because

    a.     the United States prohibits travel to certain parts of the world.
    b.     governments of other countries may prohibit travel to certain parts of the world.
    c.     other governments do not want to be embarrassed or to have politically sensitive issues revealed.
    d.     all of the above

5.     One of the most important parts of anthropological fieldwork is

    a.     fluently speaking the language of the people with whom you work.
    b.     having access to doctors trained in the United States.
    c.     being able to return home for visits every six months.
    d.     having adequate access to food from the United States.

6.     Anthropologists have written general ethnographies in the past

    a.     and today still write one in order to receive a Ph.D. but conduct more specific research to publish as books.
    b.     but today are likely to conduct more focused and problem oriented research.
    c.     and still usually use functionalist theory as the guide for their first experience of field research.
    d.     and continue to always describe every ethnographic detail of the culture they study.

7.     In the Kenya Kinship Study,

    a.     there were no independent and dependent variables.
    b.     the hypothesis was that urbanization strengthens ties to distant kin and unrelated people.
    c.     the conclusion was that living in the urban area of Nairobi does not itself lead to the truncation of extended kinship ties.
    d.     the conclusion was that living in the rural areas of Kenya does not itself lead to the truncation of extended kinship ties.

8.    The Kenya Kinship Study used which of the following research methods?

    a.    mapping
    b.    day history
    c.    unstructured interviews
    d.    all of the above

9.    Participant-observation is often used by anthropologists

    a.    and requires being involved in the culture.
    b.    and requires systematic observations of what goes on.
    c.    to allow them to experience the behavior and the social interaction they study.
    d.    all of the above
    e.    a and c

10.    Anthropologists can distinguish between normative and real behavior because of

    a.    participant-observation.
    b.    mapping.
    c.    photography.
    d.    none of the above.

11.    Unlike a psychological or a sociological interview, an ethnographic interview

    a.    is always confidential.
    b.    seldom focuses on the experiences of a single individual.
    c.    usually occurs between an interviewer and a subject who have different first languages.
    d.    b and c

12.    While anthropology students can learn about other cultures from ethnographic films, this medium also

    a.    can record information on rituals that can then be analyzed in detail at a later date.
    b.    can help anthropologists to study how people in different cultures distance themselves from one another in normal interaction.
    c.    can help in event analysis.
    d.    all of the above
    e.    a and c

13.     In anthropological research, validity is important

    a.     and can be checked by comparing people's actual behavior with the answers they have given in interviews.
    b.     but can never be tested in studies involving human interaction.
    c.     but not as important as reliability.
    d.     a and c

14.     Anthropologists, when doing fieldwork in another society,

    a.     often experience culture shock.
    b.     may be unsure of the local cultural rules for behavior.
    c.     may be afraid of being rejected by the people with whom they want to work.
    d.     all of the above
    e.     none of the above, if the anthropologists have been adequately prepared to do field research

15.     One positive result of the experience of research in another society is

    a.     immunity from culture shock.
    b.     guaranteed employment.
    c.     biculturalism, meaning an awareness of alternative ways of doing things.
    d.     all of the above

16.     Narrative anthropology

    a.     focuses on the interaction between ethnographers and their informants.
    b.     focuses of well-written scientific descriptions of other cultures.
    c.     produces conscious reflections on how anthropologists' personalities and culture combine with personal encounters with their informants to produce cultural data.
    d.     all of the above
    e.     a and c

17.     The experiential nature of anthropology means

    a.     field work always requires experiments on people.
    b.     that the use of participant-observation allows anthropologists first hand experience with the people being studied.
    c.     experiments on animals allows anthropologists to predict what humans will do.
    d.     all of the above

18.    It is very important for anthropologists to

    a.    be flexible in case the techniques originally planned in the research proposal prove to be inappropriate.
    b.    decide on what methods they will use prior to leaving for their field site.
    c.    decide on a single research method to use throughout their fieldwork.
    d.    a and b

19.    The AIDS epidemic is particularly difficult to get under control because

    a.    the disease attacks the very complex human immune system.
    b.    the viruses thought to cause the disease are poorly understood.
    c.    cultural factors related to high-risk populations.
    d.    all of the above

20.    The ethnographic study of adolescent crack cocaine dealers in Florida suggests intervention strategies must include ways of

    a.    improving the vocational and education skills of adolescents to they will have more access to legitimate work.
    b.    treating the chemical dependency of most of the drug dealers.
    c.    reducing the drug dealers' families constant demands for money.
    d.    all of the above

**TRUE-FALSE**

_____ 1.    The validity of anthropological data can be checked by asking a number of people the same question.

_____ 2.    During his fieldwork Ferraro spent some time showing teenage boys how to shoot a fifteen-foot jump shot.

_____ 3.    Participant-observation is an unobtrusive method.

_____ 4.    One of the most difficult research steps for anthropologists is interpreting their findings.

_____ 5.    Ethnographic films can provide a lasting record of land-use patterns and document the technology of the culture.

_____ 6.    Learning language is a very important part of preparing for and conducting anthropological fieldwork.

_____ 7.    The genealogical method is used to collect information on religion.

_____ 8.    Anthropologists, in their research, only develop hypotheses, not independent and dependent variables.

_____ 9.    There are very strict lists of the types of data that all anthropologists must collect when doing ethnographic fieldwork.

_____ 10.    Anthropologists benefit from securing permission to do research from the top down in the political hierarchy of their host country.

_____ 11.    People in other societies never object to photographs of public settings but frequently prevent the use of cameras in households.

_____ 12.    The fieldworker works with people who well deserve the position of teacher/expert and when that position is recognized they are likely to be willing to share their knowledge.

_____ 13.    The Kenya Kinship Study concluded that lack of money and economic security influenced family interaction in both urban and rural Kenya.

_____ 14.    While map making is necessary for anthropologists, they seldom learn much about culture from this experience.

_____ 15.    Anthropologists tend to have rather narrow views of human behavior.

_____ 16.    Anthropological research with drug-dealing youth showed that 65% of them currently used cocaine and most contributed less than 10% of their income to their families.

_____ 17.    Few fieldwork projects include formulating a research design, analyzing data, and interpreting data.

_____ 18.    All anthropologists use the same methods to collect data during fieldwork.

_____ 19.    Cultural anthropologists today seldom include very explicit discussions of how they did their fieldwork.

_____ 20.    Cultural anthropologists can make significant contributions to programs of preventative education by conducting ethnographic research on the cultural pattern of sexual behavior among groups at high-risk for AIDS.

## MATCHING

Match the following

a.    Nairobi, Kenya
b.    urbanization
c.    urbanization reduces contact with extended kin
d.    urbanization does not reduce contact with extended kin
e.    urban Kikuyu
f.    family interaction
g.    rural Kikuyu
h.    rural migration
i.    rural migration reduces contact with extended kin
j.    rural migration does not reduce contact with extended kin

1.    _____ dependent variable
2.    _____ independent variable
3.    _____ subjects of research
4.    _____ hypothesis
5.    _____ site of anthropological fieldwork
6.    _____ conclusion

## SHORT ANSWER

1.    What is the most important anthropological method?  What are its advantages over other social science methods?

2.    How do anthropologists prepare to work overseas?  What is their relationship with their host government?

3.    What are the five basic stages of fieldwork?

4.     What is the experience of culture shock like?

5.     What are additional anthropological methods anthropologists used?

# CHAPTER
# 6
# LANGUAGE

## LEARNING OBJECTIVES

Complete the work in this chapter of the Study Guide to improve your understanding of the following objectives. Read them before you begin and after you have finished the definitions and questions. Write a note to yourself about any objective that is still not clear, reread your text's discussion of that topic, and if you continue to have questions, discuss the issue with your classmates and instructor.

Having read and studied Chapter 6, you should be able to:

1. Discuss the importance of language in human culture, especially as it relates to humans' ability to adapt to a wide variety of environments.

2. Define the term language and distinguish between human and nonhuman communication in terms of closed and open systems, physical ability, and the characteristic of displacement.

3. Recognize the differences among phonological, morphological, and grammatical structures.

4. Define and give examples of phonemes and morphemes.

5. Explain the relationships among phonemes, morphemes, and grammar.

6.     Explain why, while all languages have distinct grammars, none are superior in an absolute sense to others in expression of abstract ideas.

7.     Recognize that size of and specialization in vocabulary reflects adaptive importance to a culture.

8.     Discuss the Sapir-Whorf hypothesis and the difficulties of testing it.

9.     Explain the power of language to alter people's perceptions.

10.    Discuss how a language reveals a culture's basic value structure.

11.    Describe the subject of sociolinguistics and understand its importance for everyday interactions in society.

12.    Explain the meaning of diglossia, describe when it occurs, and contrast diglossia with the use of dialects.

13.    Recognize the symbolic role of language in the development of national and ethnic identities.

14.    Explain the importance of non-verbal communication, including hand gestures, posture, and touching, for humans and the possibilities of cross-cultural misunderstanding.

## DEFINITIONS AND EXAMPLES

Write out your own definitions and examples from memory.

Define

1.     bound morpheme

_____
_____
_____

2.     closed system of communication

_____
_____
_____

3.   cultural emphasis of a language

_____

_____

_____

4.   diglossia

_____

_____

_____

5.   displacement

_____

_____

_____

6.   free morpheme

_____

_____

_____

7.   grammar

_____

_____

_____

8.   language

_____

_____

_____

9.   morphology

_____

_____

_____

10.   nonverbal communication

_____

_____

_____

11.    open system of communication

_____

_____

_____

12.    phoneme

_____

_____

_____

13.    phonology

_____

_____

_____

14.    Sapir-Whorf hypothesis

_____

_____

_____

15.    syntax

_____

_____

_____

16.    linguistic "melting pot"

_____

_____

_____

17.    Black English Vernacular (BEV)

_____

_____

_____

18.    Standard English

_____

_____

_____

19.    level two English

_____
_____
_____

## MULTIPLE-CHOICE

1.    Human's ability to communicate symbolically is important in

    a.    management of technology.
    b.    political activities.
    c.    religious activities.
    d.    all of the above

2.    Hand gestures and touch are examples of

    a.    nonverbal communication.
    b.    bound morphemes.
    c.    phonemes.
    d.    an open call system.

3.    Language communities

    a.    are approximately the same for the ten most frequently spoken languages.
    b.    vary widely in size.
    c.    of all other languages are less than half the size of the Mandarin Chinese community.
    d.    b and c

4.    The number of discrete languages that exist is

    a.    more than five thousand.
    b.    one hundred and forty-two.
    c.    two hundred and eleven.
    d.    one thousand.

5.    Linguistic displacement means

    a.    not being with other people who speak your own language.
    b.    being able to speak about things that are not present.
    c.    not sharing a language of the group with which you live.
    d.    losing your original language.

6.    Language

    a.    is a symbolic system of sound.
    b.    conveys meaning to its speakers.
    c.    has meanings attached to sounds totally arbitrarily.
    d.    all of the above
    e.    a and b

7.    The phonemes of a language limit

    a.    the number of stories told.
    b.    the number of sounds made in speech.
    c.    the number of words spoken.
    d.    none of the above

8.    The morphemes of a language convey

    a.    a sound system.
    b.    meaning.
    c.    the structure of the language.
    d.    the complete set of rules of the language.

9.    An example of a free morpheme is _____.

    a.    am
    b.    im
    c.    pre
    d.    ing

10.    An example of a bound morpheme is _____.

    a.    slime
    b.    green
    c.    ist
    d.    car

11.    The rules which govern the formation of words and sentences are

    a.    the grammar.
    b.    the script.
    c.    the dialogue.
    d.    the phonology.

12.     Displacement means

    a.     communication about particular things in the present.
    b.     the transmission of language largely through tradition.
    c.     humans' ability to speak of purely hypothetical things, not present and not happening now.
    d.     a and b

13.     Language and culture are closely related

    a.     and language learning requires learning of culture.
    b.     and the study of culture is very difficult without knowledge of its language.
    c.     but languages can be learned without the study of culture.
    d.     a and b

14.     Until the turn of the century, European linguists thought that Western languages were superior to all others in efficiency and beauty

    a.     but today there is evidence that the languages of preliterate people are the most efficient and beautiful.
    b.     but today there is evidence that Western languages have a diminishing capacity for expressing abstract ideas that has accompanied their increased emphasis on technology.
    c.     but anthropological research has shown that people from technologically simple societies are no less capable of expressing a wide variety of abstract ideas than people from high-technology societies.
    d.     a and b

15.     The argument that language influences and perhaps determines culture

    a.     is obviously wrong.
    b.     has been proven true.
    c.     is the Sapir-Whorf hypothesis.
    d.     b and c

16.     The use of terms like *outplaced, down-sized,* and *re-engineered* demonstrate

    a.     the power of language.
    b.     alters people's perceptions of various experiences.
    c.     double-speak.
    d.     all of the above
    e.     a and b

17.     Open systems of communication

    a.     are those languages which allow you to talk openly.
    b.     have sounds that are unique in form and purpose.
    c.     are capable of sending messages that have never been sent before.
    d.     were used by human ancestors before they became able to think abstract thoughts.

18.     Recent studies of nonhuman primate communication suggest that chimps and gorillas

    a.     have less advanced powers of reasoning than had been believed earlier.
    b.     do in fact have more advanced powers of reasoning than had been believed earlier.
    c.     communicate as well with verbally as they do with gestures.
    d.     b and c

19.     Black English Vernacular is

    a.     nothing more than street talk.
    b.     incorrect English.
    c.     a full-fledged linguistic system with its own grammatical rules, phonology, and semantics.
    d.     a and b

20.     Bannock-Shoshoni Native American women from the Fort Hall reservation in Idaho

    a.     speak no English.
    b.     understood level three English.
    c.     misunderstood social service regulations concerning eligibility for supplemental security income.
    d.     b and c

## TRUE-FALSE

____ 1.     Learning the meaning attached to different body postures is a distinctive process from learning other aspects of a culture.

____ 2.     Diglossia refers to an inability to speak.

____ 3.     The Nuer vocabulary indicates the importance of cattle herding in their culture.

____ 4.     It is impossible to establish the precise number of discrete languages found in the world today.

_____ 5.    Black Vernacular English is a fully efficient language with its own grammar.

_____ 6.    The Sapir-Whorf hypothesis argues that language reflects rather than determines culture.

_____ 7.    Languages use totally different, and equally arbitrary, words to describe the same things.

_____ 8.    A major limitation to the development of language among gorillas and chimpanzee is their lack of vocal equipment for speech.

_____ 9.    Displacement means losing the traditional language of your ancestors.

_____ 10.   Language can be used by large organization and government, as well as by individuals, to mislead by making things appear better than they actually are.

_____ 11.   Although individualism is important to North Americans, its significance is not reflected in Standard American English.

_____ 12.   Nonstandard English is English spoken without regard to any rules of grammar.

_____ 13.   Local languages in ethnically diverse countries in this decade are almost always supported by national governments.

_____ 14.   The difference between a young adult's speech in a college classroom and her speech to her friends in the college union would be of interest to a sociolinguist.

_____ 15.   All distinct languages have unique alphabets.

_____ 16.   Symbolic communication is important in family relationships.

_____ 17.   There is bitter conflict over official language policy in Spain and Canada.

_____ 18.   Nonverbal communication is less common in humans than in other species.

_____ 19.   A federal court in Michigan concluded that Ann Arbor schools had to develop strategies to inform the teachers how best to teach Standard English to children who enter the schools speaking Black English Vernacular.

_____ 20.   Native American women who speak English are able to talk to social service personnel and can understand their agency's rules.

**SHORT ANSWER**

1.     Why does the text say that the use of language is the most distinctive hallmark of humanity?

2.     What is the difference between open and closed systems of communication?  Which species use which forms?

3.     What is displacement?  Give an example.

4.     What is the difference between a morpheme and a phoneme?  Give an example of each.

5.     Explain the Sapir-Whorf Hypothesis.

6.     What is a grammar?  Explain why languages, while having distinct grammars, are never absolutely superior in their expression of abstract ideas.

7.     Explain what sociolinguistic is and why the study of everyday interactions is important.

8.     Describe the variety of forms nonverbal communication can take.

# CHAPTER
## 7
# GETTING FOOD

## LEARNING OBJECTIVES

Complete the work in this chapter of the Study Guide to improve your understanding of the following objectives. Read them before you begin and after you have finished the definitions and questions. Write a note to yourself about any objective that is still not clear, reread your text's discussion of that topic, and if you continue to have questions, discuss the issue with your classmates and instructor.

Having read and studied Chapter 7, you should be able to:

1.      Identify five major food-procurement categories found among the world's populations.

2.      Discuss the impact of a culture's environment and technology on its food acquisition strategies.

3.      Explain the concept of carrying capacity, the consequences of exceeding it, and the theory of optimal foraging.

4.      Describe four characteristics of the food collection strategy.

5.      Recognize the different degrees of reliability of food collection strategies and the relative success of groups in environments with stable food supplies.

6.    Compare !Kung and Inuit food collection strategies.

7.    Understand the cultural changes brought about by the Neolithic Revolution.

8.    Know what horticulture is and explain the limitations and the advantages of slash and burn cultivation.

9.    Describe the differences between transhumance and nomadic pastoralism.

10.    Understand how the change from horticulture to agriculture allowed the development of peasantry.

11.    Recognize the expenses, as well as the benefits, of industrialized agriculture, especially in terms of environmental impact.

12.    Explain the scientific rationality which people have developed because of the systematic observations required by their successful adaptation to their environments.


## DEFINITIONS AND EXAMPLES

Write out your own definitions and examples from memory.  Compare your answers with those in the book's glossary after defining all of the terms.

Define

1.    agriculture

_____

_____

_____


2.    carrying capacity

_____

_____

_____


3.    horticulture

_____

_____

_____

4.     food collecting

_____
_____
_____

5.     industrialization

_____
_____
_____

6.     Neolithic Revolution

_____
_____
_____

7.     nomadism

_____
_____
_____

8.     optimal foraging theory

_____
_____
_____

9.     pastoralism

_____
_____
_____

10.    peasantry

_____
_____
_____

11.    slash and burn

_____
_____
_____

12.    shifting cultivation

_____

_____

_____

13.    swidden cultivation

_____

_____

_____

14.    social uses of cattle

_____

_____

_____

15.    transhumance

_____

_____

_____

16.    the !Kung

_____

_____

_____

17.    the Inuit

_____

_____

_____

19.    the Bemba

_____

_____

_____

## MULTIPLE-CHOICE

1.  While agriculture is important in the contemporary world, the food-getting strategy utilized by humans for the longest period of time is

    a.  horticulture.
    b.  food collecting.
    c.  pastoralism.
    d.  slash and burn.

2.  Domesticated animals are part of which subsistence strategy?

    a.  agriculture
    b.  horticulture
    c.  pastoralism
    d.  all of the above
    e.  a and c

3.  Foragers tend to maximize their caloric return for the time spent in food procurement and

    a.  always use all nutritious materials in the environment.
    b.  make rational decisions about food procurement in light of the often sophisticated knowledge they have about plants and animals.
    c.  improve their use of the environment when scientific education becomes available to the group.
    d.  always hunt all of the types of animals suitable as meat found in their environment.

4.  The food collectors of the 1990s are found in

    a.  South America.
    b.  Europe.
    c.  Southeast Asia.
    d.  remote and marginally useful areas of the earth.
    e.  all of the above.

5.  The Inuit

    a.  are food collectors.
    b.  rely primarily on hunting and fishing.
    c.  live in smaller groups during the summer than in the winter.
    d.  all of the above

6.   Pastoralists

   a.   are always nomadic.
   b.   always have a permanent settlement.
   c.   may herd reindeer, camels, goats, llamas, sheep, donkey, horses, or cattle.
   d.   a and c

7.   Horticulturalists

   a.   use only tools driven by animals not by machines.
   b.   usually have no surplus.
   c.   usually have a significant surplus.
   d.   expend considerable energy in enriching their land.
   e.   a and c

8.   The Somali herders

   a.   have nomadic hamlets with sheep and goats.
   b.   live in either permanent settlements with cattle or the nomadic camel camp.
   c.   train young boys in camel camps which include only kin related through the male line.
   d.   a and c

9.   The difference between horticulture and agriculture is that

   a.   horticulture is a more intensive cultivation of crops.
   b.   agriculture produces a higher yield per acre and is more intensive.
   c.   irrigation is used more often in horticulture.
   d.   animal husbandry is more important in horticulture.

10.   Agriculture

   a.   relies on animal power which horticulture does not utilize.
   b.   usually uses irrigation and/or fertilizers to increase production.
   c.   requires a greater investment of labor and capital than horticulture.
   d.   all of the above
   e.   b and c

11.     Peasants

    a.      are politically tied to the city or the state.
    b.      are economically independent.
    c.      exchange surplus for goods produced in other parts of the state.
    d.      all of the above
    e.      a and c

12.     The Neolithic Revolution means

    a.      the shift from collecting to producing food.
    b.      the population explosion that preceded the shift to food production.
    c.      the change in technology from simple to complex that brought about the development of plow agriculture.
    d.      b and c

13.     Foragers

    a.      are always chronically undernourished.
    b.      may today live in villages, hunt with guns, and have TVs and telephones.
    c.      seldom experience seasonal fluctuations in their dietary intake.
    d.      all of the above
    e.      b and c

14.     Industrialized agriculture

    a.      requires relatively complex systems of market exchange because of its highly specialized nature.
    b.      is primarily carried out for subsistence.
    c.      produces only goods sold to non-agriculturists for some form of currency.
    d.      a and c

15.     Large-scale agriculture in various parts of the world has led to

    a.      lowering of water tables.
    b.      changes in the ecology of nearby bodies of surface water.
    c.      the pollution of aquifers by pesticides.
    d.      all of the above

16.    In the past, foragers

    a.    occupied remote habitats and did not have contact with nonforaging peoples.
    b.    occupied remote habitats but did have contact with nonforaging peoples.
    c.    did not participate in trade with neighboring groups.
    d.    had no involvement with neighboring military conflicts.

17.    The Bemba

    a.    plant a wide range of crops which they tend as horticulturalists.
    b.    are food collectors.
    c.    are a large and highly politically organized ethnic group in the Congo, formerly
          known as Zambia.
    d.    a and c

18.    Foragers, pastoralists and horticulturalists

    a.    never have scientific knowledge comparable to that of a trained zoologist.
    b.    have found that short-term overgrazing can actually enhance the grass on which
          the cattle feed .
    c.    limit scientifically valid knowledge about food collecting and producing to male
          members.
    d.    b and c

19.    The Tanzanian Livestock Project

    a.    began with a firm understanding of the social importance of cattle to pastoralists,
          but did not recognize the conflicts it would create in relation to traditional gender
          roles and inheritance customs.
    b.    was rapidly accepted because of the anthropologist's appraisal.
    c.    would only be successful if the social organization of the Ujamaa ranches provided
          appropriate alternatives for the many traditional social uses of cattle.
    d.    attempted to improve the subsistence cattle herding and the nutrition of the rural
          population.

20.     The South American tropical rainforest

    a.      has contributed plants from which are derived about half of all prescription drugs sold in the United States.
    b.      has contributed ethnobotanical knowledge which has allowed the production of a significant amount of the prescription drugs sold in the United States.
    c.      is inhabited by indigenous people who know more about the plants and their healing properties than Western medicine does.
    d.      all of the above
    e.      a and c

**TRUE-FALSE**

_____ 1.     There is no single type of society best able to cope with its environment.

_____ 2.     Only industrialized societies can survive for long if their level of production exceeds their environment's carrying capacity.

_____ 3.     The diet of the Bemba, food collectors of the former Zambia, alternate between scarcity and plenty.

_____ 4.     Most anthropologists agree that pure pastoralists, those who get all their food from livestock, are relatively common.

_____ 5.     A fully efficient system of food production brought about by intensive agriculture is a necessary, if not sufficient, condition for the rise of civilization.

_____ 6.     A surplus of food is necessary for a society to survive.

_____ 7.     The !Kung of southern Africa work many more hours a week as food collectors than do people who are farmers.

_____ 8.     The Inuit live in large communities of several distantly related extended families while hunting seals on the surface of ice during the summer.

_____ 9.     Powerful urban populations, through the use of force or military power, often extract both labor and products from peasants in the form of taxation, rent, or tribute.

_____ 10.    A society's technology determines the carrying capacity of its environment.

_____ 11.    Peasants, because they are rural populations, are not subject to the laws and controls of the state.

_____ 12.     The average !Kung spends 12 to 19 hours a week in pursuit of food.

_____ 13.     Approximately 15,000 years ago people began to domesticate plants and animals.

_____ 14.     Industrialists are best able to cope with their environment.

_____ 15.     Inuit today no longer engage in traditional hunting and fishing.

_____ 16.     Pastoral societies generally control territory that is not able to support any type of cultivation.

_____ 17.     Agricultural products in industrialized societies is largely sold by food producers to nonproducers.

_____ 18.     Because they usually supply their society with most of its food, peasants have high social status and significant political power.

_____ 19.     Industrialized societies, while producing great amounts of food, do not necessarily distribute it to all members of their society nor take good care of their environment.

_____ 20.     Like horticulture, agriculture is usually associated with permanent settlements and high levels of labor specialization.

_____ 21.     The Tanzanian Livestock Project attempted to commercialize livestock providing capital to individual families and an increasing the food supply for domestic consumption and export.

_____ 22.     For thousands of years indigenous people have built a storehouse of knowledge about the curative properties of plants which is being lost as they lose their land, their languages, and their cultures.

## MATCHING

Match the following.

a.     horticulture
b.     pastoralism
c.     agriculture
d.     industrialization
e.     food collecting

1.   _____   first type of food-getting strategy to support a state society
2.   _____   carried out in environment that will not support the growing of crops
3.   _____   usually meat or animal products are traded for grain products
4.   _____   supports large population with a small proportion working in food production
5.   _____   supports the largest number of specialized labor roles
6.   _____   raises crops but not domestic animals
7.   _____   seldom supports groups of people larger than 25
8.   _____   uses fossil fuels in food production
9.   _____   uses slash and burn technique
10.  _____   people work fewest hours a week at food procurement

## SHORT ANSWER

1.     Describe the five major food procurement categories recognized by cultural anthropologists.

2.     How does technology, as a part of culture, help humans adapt to environments?

3.     What is optimal foraging theory?

4.     Describe the concept of carrying capacity.

5.     Why do anthropologists say that environments generally set broad limits rather than determine food-getting practices?

6.     How are food collecting and pastoralist societies similar?  How do they differ?

7.     How are horticultural and agricultural societies similar?  How do they differ?

8.     How is industrialization a distinct system of food production from all others?  What is similar to other strategies?

9.     What have been the social and political consequences of the development of agriculture?

10.    Why do people in all food-getting strategies develop scientific rationality?

# CHAPTER
# 8
# ECONOMICS

## LEARNING OBJECTIVES

Complete the work in this chapter of the Study Guide to improve your understanding of the following objectives. Read them before you begin and after you have finished the definitions and questions. Write a note to yourself about any objective that is still not clear, reread your text's discussion of that topic, and if you continue to have questions, discuss the issue with your classmates and instructor.

Having read and studied Chapter 8, you should be able to:

1.   Explain the focus of cross-cultural studies of economics.

2.   Understand the distinct positions of substantivists and formalists.

3.   Recognize that there are alternative ways of allocating natural resources other than the principle of private property.

4.   Describe the advantages of community control of resources for hunters and gatherers, pastoralists, and horticulturalists.

5.   Explain the significance of the concepts of production, distribution, and consumption for anthropological economics.

6.    Recognize the importance of the study of division of labor, especially in non-industrialized societies.

7.    Explain the universal use of gender and age for allocation of economic tasks.

8.    Distinguish among three types of reciprocity.

9.    Understand the difference between redistribution and market economy.

10.    Explain the differences between the economic roles of big men and chiefs.

11.    Present a clear description of the variety of markets that exist and their distinct functions.

## DEFINITIONS AND EXAMPLES

Write out your own definitions and examples from memory.  Compare your answers with those in the book's glossary after defining all of the terms.

Define

1.    allocation of resources

_____

_____

_____


2.    balanced reciprocity

_____

_____

_____


3.    barter

_____

_____

_____


4.    big men

_____

_____

_____

5.     bridewealth

_____

_____

_____


6.     capital goods

_____

_____

_____


7.     consumer goods

_____

_____

_____


8.     division of labor

_____

_____

_____


9.     economic anthropology

_____

_____

_____


10.    economics

_____

_____

_____


11.    formalists

_____

_____

_____


12.    generalized reciprocity

_____

_____

_____

13.     kula ring

_____
_____
_____

14.     market exchange

_____
_____
_____

15.     mechanical solidarity

_____
_____
_____

16.     negative reciprocit

_____
_____
_____

17.     organic solidarity

_____
_____
_____

18.     potlatch

_____
_____
_____

19.     production

_____
_____
_____

20.     property rights

_____
_____
_____

21.     reciprocity

_____
_____
_____

22.     redistribution

_____
_____
_____

23.     silent trade

_____
_____
_____

24.     substantive approach

_____
_____
_____

## MULTIPLE-CHOICE

1.     All societies must develop systems of

   a.     distribution.
   b.     production.
   c.     consumption.
   d.     all of the above

2.     Studies of industrialized, Western societies have produced _____ theory.

   a.     substantivist
   b.     functionalist
   c.     structuralist
   d.     formalist

3.     The idea that people, when exchanging goods and services, naturally strive to maximize their material well-being and their profits is part of what theory?

   a.     substantivist
   b.     functionalist
   c.     structuralist
   d.     formalist

4. The anthropologists that argue that nonwestern societies operate on economic principles distinct from those of industrialized societies are

   a. substantivists.
   b. functionalists.
   c. structuralists.
   d. formalists.

5. The anthropologists who argue that nonwestern societies operate on the same economic principles as those of industrialized societies are

   a. substantivists.
   b. functionalists.
   c. structuralists.
   d. formalists.

6. Allocation of resources

   a. has created private ownership of most of the world's private property.
   b. determines systematic ways for allocating land among members of societies.
   c. includes public ownership of many utility companies in the United States.
   d. all of the above
   e. b and c

7. Extended kinship groups usually control horticulturalists'

   a. kitchens.
   b. food products.
   c. lands.
   d. all of the above
   e. a and b

8. Horticulturalists,

   a. like pastoralists, communally control land.
   b. like food collectors, communally control land.
   c. because they are often shifting cultivators, would have no advantage to claiming ownership over land.
   d. all of the above

9.      The concept of production includes

    a.      weaving cloth on a hand loom for oneself.
    b.      weaving cloth in a factory.
    c.      baking cookies for sale.
    d.      building houses for one's kin.
    e.      all of the above

10.     Culture influences production in the United States by

    a.      defining dogs and cats as inedible.
    b.      making potatoes a popular food.
    c.      defining a variety of meats as a desirable food.
    d.      all of the above
    e.      b and c

11.     The idea that, in terms of reproduction, men tend to be more expendable than women

    a.      is ridiculous.
    b.      may influence the division of labor by gender.
    c.      is wrong because it is only political and historical forces that determine gender roles in all societies.
    d.      is wrong because it is men's greater body mass and strength that determine their gender role.

12.     An exchange of goods and/or services of almost exactly the same value that occurs over a short period of time is

    a.      generalized reciprocity.
    b.      balanced reciprocity.
    c.      negative reciprocity.
    d.      redistribution.

13.     Anthropological market research developed

    a.      an "unfocus" technique to discover unconscious cultural codes and assumptions about a product.
    b.      techniques designed to learn what people actually do rather than what they say they do.
    c.      the technique of interviewing people randomly in shopping malls.
    d.      all of the above
    e.      a and b

14.    Generalized reciprocity

   a.    carries a high level of moral obligation.
   b.    usually involves family or close friends.
   c.    may continue between parents and children after the children are adults.
   d.    all of the above

15.    In the United States the dominant form of exchange is

   a.    generalized reciprocity.
   b.    market exchange.
   c.    negative reciprocity.
   d.    redistribution.

16.    The exchange of goods and services between two partners in generalized reciprocity

   a.    involves only immediate exchange of equivalent goods and services.
   b.    involves formal relationships and greater social distance.
   c.    only a moderate obligation to repay the original "gift."
   d.    all of the above

17.    The concept of negative reciprocity

   a.    involves the greatest desire for personal gain.
   b.    may involve cheating or theft.
   c.    involves the least personal social relations.
   d.    all of the above
   e.    a and c

18.    Subsistence production

   a.    creates goods primarily for rural markets.
   b.    is a form of redistribution of goods by a local political leader.
   c.    is found in economies which produce for survival rather than for the market.
   d.    allows a formal redistribution of goods to family members by young men returning from work in the city.

19.    Bureaucratic organizations in industrialized societies

    a.    always respect strong kinship ties and obligations.
    b.    expect that conduct between two people is determined by a universally applicable set of rules and not personal status.
    c.    expect that conduct between two people is determined by personal status and not a universally applicable set of rules.
    d.    a and c

20.    Research on two companies in Kenya

    a.    found that production was high because they had developed a universally applicable set of rules for on-the-job behavior.
    b.    that recruited new workers on the basis of kinship relations with the present workers or ethnic identity found that productivity was not harmed.
    c.    found that ethnic/kinship homogenization damaged the organization.
    d.    b and c

**TRUE-FALSE**

____ 1.    The household is the basic unit of production in many societies.

____ 2.    Economic anthropologists study production, distribution and consumption in non-industrialized and industrialized societies.

____ 3.    Tribute includes gifts of food and other material goods to tribal chiefs from their constituents.

____ 4.    Market exchanges are primarily social in nature.

____ 5.    Market economies always require standardized currency.

____ 6.    Gender roles may be defined in such a way that females and males do not do the work of which they are capable.

____ 7.    All societies have a division of labor based on age.

____ 8.    The turnover rates fell to less than half when two companies in Kenya experienced more ethnic and kinship homogenization.

____ 9.    Negative reciprocity is most common within households.

____ 10.    Balanced reciprocity requires face-to-face contact among those involved.

____ 11.    The Kwakiutl Indians' potlatch is a form of balanced reciprocity.

____ 12.    Market economies are always highly impersonal.

____ 13.    Distribution includes bridewealth, potlatch, and tribute paid to an African chief.

____ 14.    Durkheim's concept of mechanical solidarity is based on commonality of interests and social homogeneity.

____ 15.    Food collectors' reciprocity is adaptive because it serves to increase the chances of survival of all members of the society.

____ 16.    Pastoralists always maintain communal control of water and pasturage.

____ 17.    The same types of tasks may be associated with the opposite gender in different societies.

____ 18.    The notion of private property is the dominant way of thinking in almost all societies.

____ 19.    Major corporations have found anthropological research useful in their efforts to learn how and why people use or fail to use certain products.

____ 20.    Anthropological research has shown that it would be beneficial to both the corporate organization and its workforce to experiment with different organizational structures that take into account the realities of the local cultures.

____ 21.    Production means a process whereby goods are obtained from the natural environment and altered to become goods consumed by members of a society.

____ 22.    Tribute includes the Trobriand Island Kula Ring.

## SHORT ANSWER

1.    How is economic anthropology different from the discipline of economics?

2.    What are the positions of the substantivists and formalists and how do they disagree?

3.    What are alternative ways of allocating natural resources other than the principle of private property?

4.    Define production, distribution, and consumption.

5.    What are two universal forms of division of labor?

6.    Describe three types of reciprocity.

7.    What is a market system?  How is it different from redistribution?

8.    In what economies is the household the basic unit of production?  How is household production different than that of a business firm?

# CHAPTER
# 9
# KINSHIP AND DESCENT

## LEARNING OBJECTIVES

Complete the work in this chapter of the Study Guide to improve your understanding of the following objectives. Read them before you begin and after you have finished the definitions and questions. Write a note to yourself about any objective that is still not clear, reread your text's discussion of that topic, and if you continue to have questions, discuss the issue with your classmates and instructor.

Having read and studied Chapter 9, you should be able to:

1.  Explain how the complexity of human social organization differs from that of any other species.

2.  Contrast the importance of kinship as a factor in the social structure of small-scale societies with its importance in industrialized societies.

3.  Give a clear definition of kinship.

4.  Recognize the importance of cultural rules for kinship classification that may not account for biological factors.

5.  Diagram your own or others' kinship systems.

6.  Describe how sex and age are important in determining kinship relationships.

7.    Explain the structure of both patrilineal and matrilineal descent systems.

8.    Understand the organizational hierarchy of moieties, phratries, clans, and lineages.

9.    Describe the three types of cognatic descent and explain what is a bilateral system's kindred.

10.    Explain the six basic systems of classification.

## DEFINITIONS AND EXAMPLES

Write out your own definitions and examples from memory.  Compare your answers with those in the book's glossary after defining all of the terms.

Define

1.    kinship

_____
_____
_____

2.    descent

_____
_____
_____

3.    gender

_____
_____
_____

4.    collaterality

_____
_____
_____

5.    ambilineal descent

_____
_____
_____

6.    bilateral descent

_____

_____

_____

7.    clan

_____

_____

_____

8.    cognatic descent

_____

_____

_____

9.    Crow system

_____

_____

_____

10.    double descent

_____

_____

_____

11.    ego

_____

_____

_____

12.    Eskimo system

_____

_____

_____

13.    Hawaiian system

_____

_____

_____

14.   horizontal function of kinship

_____

_____

_____

15.   Iroquois system

_____

_____

_____

16.   kinship system

_____

_____

_____

17.   lineage

_____

_____

_____

18.   matriarchy

_____

_____

_____

19.   matrilineal descent

_____

_____

_____

20.   moieties

_____

_____

_____

21.   Omaha system

_____

_____

_____

22.     patrilineal descent

_____
_____
_____

23.     phratries

_____
_____
_____

24.     Sudanese system

_____
_____
_____

25.     unilineal descent

_____
_____
_____

26.     vertical function of kinship

_____
_____
_____

Give an example as well as a definition for the following:

27.     affinal relatives

_____
_____
_____
_____

28.     collaterality

_____
_____
_____
_____

29.    consanguineal relatives

_____
_____
_____
_____

30.    fictive kinship

_____
_____
_____
_____

31.    kindred

_____
_____
_____
_____

32.    lineality

_____
_____
_____
_____

## MULTIPLE-CHOICE

1.    Kinship includes

    a.    consanguineal relatives.
    b.    affinal relatives.
    c.    people, defined by culture, as blood relatives.
    d.    all of the above

2.    A fictive kin is someone who is

    a.    related to you through your great-grandparent's generation.
    b.    a parallel cousin.
    c.    a kissing cousin.
    d.    not related to you through blood or marriage.

3.    Anthropologists have studied kinship more than any other single aspect of culture because

    a.    those relationships are all-encompassing in all types of societies.
    b.    they have mostly worked in societies where those relations are tantamount to social relations.
    c.    those relationships are all-encompassing in highly urbanized, technological societies.
    d.    all of the above
    e.    a and b

4.    The way that different societies sort and categorize kinship relationships is

    a.    primarily determined by biology.
    b.    as much a matter of culture as it is of biology.
    c.    remarkably uniform across all societies.
    d.    unique in every society of the world.

5.    The ego is the

    a.    person who is the point of reference in a kinship diagram.
    b.    oldest child of the parents.
    c.    oldest ancestor of the clan.
    d.    oldest surviving kin.

6.    The vertical function of a kinship system always binds together

    a.    members of a single generation.
    b.    members of successive generations.
    c.    members of groups that exchange marriage partners.
    d.    only the male descendants of an ancestor.

7.    Kinship categories

    a.    include relatives who have no expectation about how they will be treated by relatives.
    b.    may include females and males.
    c.    include relatives who may be referred to by many different terms.
    d.    all of the above

8.      The term descent means

   a.      all of your relationships through blood or marriage.
   b.      all of your relationships through marriage and divorce.
   c.      the rules that establish affiliation with one's parents.
   d.      a and c

9.      A unilineal descent system is one in which

   a.      you have an established relationship only with your parent of the same sex.
   b.      you have no relationship whatsoever with any of your siblings of the opposite sex.
   c.      you trace descent through one parent and his/her ancestors of only one sex.
   d.      there are no marriage relationships.

10.     A patrilineal descent group

   a.      gives no roles of any significance to women.
   b.      traces descent through male, but not female, relatives.
   c.      is the most common type of descent group.
   d.      b and c

11.     A matrilineal descent group

   a.      gives no roles of any significance to men.
   b.      traces descent through female, but not male, relatives.
   c.      is the most common type of descent group.
   d.      b and c

12.     Clans are found

   a.      in all societies with moieties.
   b.      in unilineal descent systems.
   c.      in all societies with lineages.
   d.      b and c

13.     When people can trace, step-by-step, ancestry back to a common ancestor they have _____ organization.

   a.      moiety
   b.      phratry
   c.      clan
   d.      lineage

14.    The same term is used for all relatives of the same sex and generation in which system of kinship classification?

    a.    Hawaiian
    b.    Omaha
    c.    Crow
    d.    Sudanese

15.    Which systems of kinship classification are mirror images of each other's concentration on unilineal descent?

    a.    Eskimo and Hawaiian
    b.    Iroquois and Omaha
    c.    Omaha and Crow
    d.    Eskimo and Iroquois

16.    Distinguishing among kin on the basis of generation

    a.    is a characteristic of North American kinship.
    b.    puts mothers, fathers, and their siblings in the generation above ego.
    c.    puts MM, MF, FM, and FF in a single generation.
    d.    all of the above
    e.    a and b

17.    Kinship systems may distinguish among kin on the basis of

    a.    gender.
    b.    lineality versus collaterality.
    c.    relative age.
    d.    all of the above
    e.    a and b

18.    In the USAID project in the West African country of Guinea the

    a.    original design included studies of local farmers' agricultural knowledge.
    b.    participation of anthropologists in the original design of the project ensured its smooth success.
    c.    original project design assumed that modern technology from the United States would transform the rural area.
    d.    first stage was a study of the sociocultural realities of the rural farmers.

19.    Research on child abuse in Kenya

     a.     shows a decrease in incidence.
     b.     shows the detrimental effect of male migration which has reduced equally shared responsibility among males and females for premarital pregnancies.
     c.     demonstrates child abuse is a matter of individual pathology.
     d.     shows migration has had little effect on strong kinship-based communities.

20.    Bilateral descent is primarily found among

     a.     horticulturalists.
     b.     foragers.
     c.     industrialized societies.
     d.     b and c

## TRUE-FALSE

_____ 1.    In the United States, relationships are more long-term and intense among kin than non-kin.

_____ 2.    A parallel cousin is either your mother's brother or your father's brother.

_____ 3.    A division of a society into two unilineal groups produces moieties.

_____ 4.    Collateral relatives are a woman and her female children.

_____ 5.    In societies with a double descent system, members are part of both their matrilineage and their patrilineage.

_____ 6.    Cognatic descent groups have a corporate nature and control property including animals and land.

_____ 7.    In a matrilineal descent system women have greater authority and power than men.

_____ 8.    Every society defines the nature of kinship interaction by determining which kin are more socially important than others.

_____ 9.    No kinship system in the world uses a different term of reference for every single relative.

_____ 10.    A kinship diagram of a married woman, her parents and her children includes affinal relatives.

_____ 11.    Cross-culturally, most kinship systems provide links between successive generations and ties across a single generation.

_____ 12.    The North American use of the term "aunt" does not distinguish between consanguineal and affinal relationships.

_____ 13.    Human social organization is less complex than that of nonhuman primates.

_____ 14.    More societies have matrilineal than patrilineal descent groups.

_____ 15.    Matriarchies are only found in societies with matrilineal descent.

_____ 16.    A phratry is a group of related lineages.

_____ 17.    The Sudanese system of kinship classification is the most descriptive.

_____ 18.    Moieties are an excellent example of social reciprocity.

_____ 19.    Kinship in the United States is bilateral and uses the Eskimo classification system.

_____ 20.    In an ambilineal descent system, boys belong to their father's and girls to their mother's descent group.

## COMPLETION

1.    Define kinship and explain its importance for all societies.

2.    Compare the roles of biology and culture in determining kinship.

3.    What is the role of kinship in a small-scaled society?

4.    Draw a kinship chart for at least two generations of your own family.

5.    Contrast the structure of matrilineal and patrilineal kinship systems.

6.    Describe the organization of moieties, phratries, clans, and lineages.

7.    What are differences between cognatic and unilineal kinship systems?

8.    What are the six basic systems of kinship classification?  Which is found in the United States?

# CHAPTER
## 10
## MARRIAGE AND THE FAMILY

## LEARNING OBJECTIVES

Complete the work in this chapter of the Study Guide to improve your understanding of the following objectives. Read them before you begin and after you have finished the definitions and questions. Write a note to yourself about any objective that is still not clear, reread your text's discussion of that topic, and if you continue to have questions, discuss the issue with your classmates and instructor.

Having read and studied Chapter 10, you should be able to:

1.    Give a cross-culturally valid definition of family.

2.    Give a cross-culturally valid definition of marriage.

3.    Explain three functions of marriage.

4.    Define incest and summarize four theories explaining why the incest taboo is universal.

5.    Explain and give examples of endogamy and exogamy.

6.    Describe how unilineal descent systems make cousin marriages possible and often preferable.

7.    Understand the circumstances that foster the practice of polygyny.

8.   Explain the circumstances in which polyandry occurs and the ways in which it is adaptive.

9.   Understand the practice of bridewealth and why it is important to recognize its social, as well as economic aspects.

10.   Describe how exchange of women as spouses between kin groups and the practice of dowry is related to the status of women in society.

11.   Understand the variety of residence patterns after marriage.

12.   Explain under what circumstances extended families are found and why they are not more common in the United States.

13.   Explain under what circumstance nuclear families are found and in which economies they are most beneficial.

14.   Describe modern-day family structure and its functions.

## DEFINITIONS AND EXAMPLES

Write out your own definitions and examples from memory. Compare your answers with those in the book's glossary after defining all of the terms.

Define

1.   ambilocal residence

   _____
   _____
   _____

2.   arranged marriage

   _____
   _____
   _____

3.   avunculocal residence

   _____
   _____
   _____

4.    bridewealth

_____

_____

_____

5.    bride service

_____

_____

_____

6.    dowry

_____

_____

_____

7.    endogamy

_____

_____

_____

8.    exogamy

_____

_____

_____

9.    incest taboo

_____

_____

_____

10.   kibbutz

_____

_____

_____

11.   levirate

_____

_____

_____

12.   matrilocal residence

_____
_____
_____

13.   monogamy

_____
_____
_____

14.   neolocal residence

_____
_____
_____

15.   patrilocal residence

_____
_____
_____

16.   polyandry

_____
_____
_____

17.   polygamy

_____
_____
_____

18.   polygyny

_____
_____
_____

19.   postpartum sex taboo

_____
_____
_____

20.    preferential cousin marriage

_____
_____
_____

21.    reciprocal exchange

_____
_____
_____

22.    role ambiguity

_____
_____
_____

23.    sororate

_____
_____
_____

24.    woman exchange

_____
_____
_____

Give an example of people in your own family who have these roles, as well as an anthropological definition for the following:

25.    cross cousins

_____
_____
_____
_____

26.    parallel cousins

_____
_____
_____
_____

27.    extended family

_____

_____

_____

_____


28.    nuclear family

_____

_____

_____

_____


## MULTIPLE-CHOICE

1.    Cross-culturally, the term family refers to

    a.    a variety of social groups.
    b.    a husband, wife, and their children.
    c.    a couple, their parents, and their children.
    d.    a woman and her children.

2.    Your textbook defines marriage as regulating socially approved

    a.    sexual and social rights and obligations between two adults.
    b.    sexual rights and obligations between a man and a woman.
    c.    social rights and obligations between a woman and a man.
    d.    b and c

3.    Same sex marriages

    a.    will never become legalized in a Western country.
    b.    are found in a number of countries around the world.
    c.    have never been found outside of Europe.
    d.    a and b

4.    Although marriage is defined as a normally permanent arrangement,

    a.    marriages last until death only in industrialized societies.
    b.    marriages last until death only in non-industrialized societies.
    c.    this is an ideal not actual fact in many societies.
    d.    impermanent marriages can also be found in smaller-scale societies.
    e.    c and d

5.      Married couples do not cohabit

     a.      in all professional families in the United States.
     b.      in many African societies.
     c.      among the Nayar of southern India.
     d.      all of the above

6.      The prohibition against sexual relations with certain categories of kin is called

     a.      monogamy.
     b.      the incest taboo.
     c.      cross-cousin marriage.
     d.      endogamy.

7.      The idea that there is a biologically harmful effect of mating between close kin is the

     a.      family disruption theory of the incest taboo.
     b.      expanding social alliance theory of the incest taboo.
     c.      inbreeding theory of the incest taboo.
     d.      none of the above

8.      The idea that by forcing people to marry outside of their immediate family they develop a wider network of interfamily alliances is the

     a.      family disruption theory of the incest taboo.
     b.      expanding social alliance theory of the incest taboo.
     c.      inbreeding theory of the incest taboo.
     d.      none of the above

9.      Choosing who one will marry

     a.      is the decision of individuals in almost all societies.
     b.      may be strongly influenced by cultural rules about marriage.
     c.      can be an important decision made by the parents of the couple.
     d.      all of the above
     e.      b and c

10.   Cross cousins marriage is

    a.     always incest.
    b.     always produces deformed children.
    c.     the preferred marriage in some societies.
    d.     a and b
    e.     none of the above

11.   Exogamy

    a.     means marrying inside a certain group.
    b.     exists in all societies because of the universality of the incest taboo.
    c.     means marrying outside of a certain group.
    d.     usually means marrying inside the lineage in unilineal descent groups.
    e/     b and c

12.   Endogamy

    a.     means marrying outside of a certain group.
    b.     exists at a high level in many complex Western societies.
    c.     is not found in societies which practice exogamy.
    d.     a and b

13.   Monogamy is

    a.     having two or more wives at the same time.
    b.     marrying the sister of your dead wife.
    c.     having one spouse at a time.
    d.     marrying the brother of your dead husband.

14.   The levirate

    a.     means marrying the brother of your dead husband.
    b.     usually determines that any children fathered by the new husband are considered to legally belong to the dead brother rather than to the actual genitor.
    c.     serves as a form of social security for the widow and her children.
    d.     all of the above

15.    Polyandry is

     a.     having more than one husband.
     b.     having more than one wife.
     c.     keeps family land intact when there is a land shortage.
     d.     a and c

16.    A reduction in the number of polygynous marriages in a society results

     a.     when women are an economic liability.
     b.     when Christian values are accepted.
     c.     if more men are available to marry than are women.
     d.     all of the above

17.    The KEEP project in Hawaii focused on

     a.     a comparison of school and home cultures as they relate to assignment and organization of tasks.
     b.     overachieving Hawaiian children in order to learn why they succeeded.
     c.     the differences between Hawaiian Creole English and Standard English.
     d.     children's uncooperativeness and laziness at home.

18.    Educational anthropologists working for KEEP in Hawaii

     a.     applied their findings to modify the culture of the family to conform to classroom culture.
     b.     applied their findings to modify the culture of the classroom to conform to students' family culture.
     c.     found the children's family culture to be almost identical to classroom culture.
     d.     found the children's family culture to be so different from the classroom culture of the schools that it was impossible to improve the children's experiences in school.

19.    Modern-day family structure in the United States

     a.     is increasingly nuclear, including a mother, father, and children.
     b.     may use extended kin in their strategy for coping with poverty.
     c.     includes less than twenty-seven percent of married couples having children under eighteen years of age.
     d.     a and b
     e.     b and c

20.    Polygyny

 a. is one form of marriage practiced by the Shipibo of South America.
 b. is the only form of marriage practiced by the Shipibo of South America today.
 c. reduced their population growth.
 d. a and c

## TRUE-FALSE

_____ 1. Some cultures consider marriage to be a union of two kin group, not just two individuals.

_____ 2. Marriage, as a socially legitimate sexual union, may limit as well as permit sexual relations between spouses.

_____ 3. Only in industrialized societies can marriages provide the material, education, and emotional needs of children for long periods of time.

_____ 4. Matrilocal residence is a couple living near the family of the bride after marriage.

_____ 5. Neolocal residence is the most common type of residence rule.

_____ 6. Bridewealth, in almost all societies, is still an exchange of commodities and not money from the groom's lineage to the bride's.

_____ 7. Polygyny is a more common marriage rule than monogamy.

_____ 8. Dowries are always given by the bride's family to the groom or his family.

_____ 9. Common residence is the only universal rule defining family.

_____ 10. Nuclear families are found in societies in which there is a great deal of geographic mobility.

_____ 11. Competition among co-wives can be reduced by establishing a hierarchy among wives.

_____ 12. The mother-infant bond has remained strong among poor families living in a shantytown in Brazil, in spite of a high level of infant mortality.

_____ 13. Most societies think that polygamy is less moral than monogamy.

_____ 14.   In the levirate, a widow is expected to marry the brother or another close relative of her dead husband.

_____ 15.   Exogamy is found only in unilineal descent systems.

_____ 16.   Endogamy is found in traditional caste societies.

_____ 17.   Polygynous societies may postpone the age at which men can marry, thereby, creating a surplus of marriageable women.

_____ 18.   Serial monogamy is very rare in the United States, Canada, and western Europe.

_____ 19.   Extended family must always be linked through parent-child bonds.

_____ 20.   Only approximately 20 percent of all U.S. families have a breadwinning husband and a homemaking wife.

## MATCHING

Match the following

a.    ambilocal residence
b.    neolocal residence
c.    exogamy
d.    endogamy
e.    parallel cousins
f.    cross cousins
g     dowry
h.    bridewealth
i.    polyandry
j.    polygyny

1.    _____    children of siblings of the same sex
2.    _____    living in a new location
3.    _____    marriage within a group
4.    _____    money given by the family of the bride
5.    _____    money given by the family of the groom
6.    _____    living with relatives of either the wife or the husband
7.    _____    marriage outside of a group
8.    _____    marriage to more than one husband
9.    _____    children of siblings of the opposite sex
10.   _____    marriage to more than one wife

## SHORT ANSWER

1.      Define family.  What is it difficult to have one definition for all cultures?


2.      Define marriage and explain three functions it has.


3.      Why is the prohibition against incest universal?


4.      Define and give examples of endogamy and exogamy.


5.      Explain the different types of marriage found cross-culturally and how they influence adaptation to environments.


6.      What are the pattern of residence after marriage?


7.      Why are nuclear families not more common in the United States?


8.      What are functions of extended families and where are such families found?

**CHAPTER
11
GENDER**

## LEARNING OBJECTIVES

Complete the work in this chapter of the Study Guide to improve your understanding of the following objectives. Read them before you begin and after you have finished the definitions and questions. Write a note to yourself about any objective that is still not clear, reread your text's discussion of that topic, and if you continue to have questions, discuss the issue with your classmates and instructor.

Having read and studied Chapter 11, you should be able to:

1.    Explain why anthropologists discuss gender differences rather than sex differences.

2.    Discuss how research on gender in other cultures demonstrates that it is not biology alone that is responsible for differences in women's and men's behavior.

3.    Understand the large variation in human sexuality across cultures.

4.    Recognize that the universal presence of gender role definitions does not mean the roles are identical in all societies.

5.    Understand the meaning of gender stratification and the difficulties involved in its measurement.

6.      Discuss the relative sexual equality in food collecting societies and suggest two reasons why that equality exists.

7.      Discuss whether or not women are universally subordinate and the dimensions in which women's status varies.

8.      Explain what gender ideology is and be able to argue whether those ideologies represent only a male perspective.

9.      Give examples of male gender bias and the impact it has on women in ours and other cultures.

10.     Discuss the controversy about genital mutilation and female infanticide.

11.     Explain when there was a period of breadwinner/housewife households in the U.S. and why that type of household came to prevail and then became less common.

12.     Describe the characteristics of occupational segregation along gender lines in the United States and the impact that has on relations of women and men.

## DEFINITIONS AND EXAMPLES

Write out your own definitions and examples from memory. Compare your answers with those in the book's glossary after defining all of the terms.

Define

1.      gender

_____
_____
_____

2.      sex

_____
_____
_____

3.      gender roles

_____
_____
_____

4.     gender stratification

_____

_____

_____

5.     gender ideology

_____

_____

_____

6.     occupational segregation

_____

_____

_____

7.     breadwinner

_____

_____

_____

8.     double work load

_____

_____

_____

9.     extramarital activity

_____

_____

_____

10.    female infanticide

_____

_____

_____

11.    femininity

_____

_____

_____

12.    feminization of poverty

_____

_____

_____

13.    genderlects

_____

_____

_____

14.    heterosexual

_____

_____

_____

15.    homosexual

_____

_____

_____

16.    housewife

_____

_____

_____

17.    human sexuality

_____

_____

_____

18.    infant mortality

_____

_____

_____

19.    male gender bias

_____

_____

_____

20.    masculinity

_____

_____

_____

21.    matriarchy

_____

_____

_____

22.    nutritional deprivation

_____

_____

_____

23.    postpartum sexual abstinence

_____

_____

_____

24.    purdah

_____

_____

_____

25.    rape

_____

_____

_____

26.    sex drive

_____

_____

_____

27.    sex roles

_____

_____

_____

28.    sexual asymmetry

_____

_____

_____

29.    sexual dimorphism

_____

_____

_____

30.    spouse abuse

_____

_____

_____

31.    subordination

_____

_____

_____

32.    universal male dominance

_____

_____

_____

## MULTIPLE-CHOICE

1.    Statistics on the status of women throughout the world reveal

    a.    that gender roles are seldom egalitarian.
    b.    that two-thirds of the illiterate people in the world today are women.
    c.    that women are increasingly part of the world's work force but are concentrated in the lowest-paid occupations.
    d.    all of the above

2.    Female subordination

    a.    is universal, although least present in industrialized societies.
    b.    is a complex topic to study because it involves a number of components that may vary independently of one another.
    c.    is not a static phenomenon.
    d.    all of the above
    e.    b and c

3.   We say that humans are sexually dimorphic because

    a.   women and men are so similar physiologically.
    b.   males have a X and a Y chromosome while women have two X chromosomes.
    c.   humans manifest obvious physiological differences between males and females.
    d.   a and b

4.   Margaret Mead's 1935 study of three New Guinea cultures illustrated that

    a.   women's temperament may vary but men are always aggressive.
    b.   men's temperament may vary but women are always nonaggressive.
    c.   men and women never have the same traits defined for each gender.
    d.   there is a tremendous range of variation in the traits defined for each gender.

5.   A combined male/female role is

    a.   pathological in all cultures.
    b.   a major theme in Hindu art, religion, and mythology.
    c.   found only in urban U.S. and European settings.
    d.   always criminal in contemporary societies.

6.   Sex and gender are

    a.   two words with the same meaning.
    b.   distinct concepts because sex is defined by cultural and gender is determined by biology.
    c.   distinct concepts because sex is a term used for animals and gender is a term used for humans.
    d.   distinct concepts because sex is determined by biology and gender is culturally defined.

7.   In many cultures, gender specific roles include

    a.   planting crops for women.
    b.   making crafts for women.
    c.   tending small domesticated animals  for women.
    d.   all of the above

8.    In spite of the biology of pregnancy and breast feeding,

      a.    a woman's work obligations may take precedence over child care considerations.
      b.    when women's work is important, men usually take over child care.
      c.    women in all societies today work outside the home.
      d.    there is remarkably little difference in gender roles in preindustrial societies.

9.    Gender stratification is

      a.    always determined by males' strength.
      b.    always independent of economic status.
      c.    determined by a number of components what may vary independently of one another.
      d.    a and b

10.   Purdah is

      a.    an ancient custom which is no longer practiced in the Middle East.
      b.    a practice which always prevents women from receiving higher education.
      c.    a practice of domestic seclusion and veiling which is not static, that is, it has governed larger and smaller groups of women over time.
      d.    a practice found in societies which are matriarchies.

11.   A matriarchy is/was

      a.    found only in the Amazon of South America.
      b.    found in only a few areas of Africa.
      c.    found in England and, in the past, in India and Israel.
      d.    never found to exist anywhere in the world, now or in the past.

12.   Genderlects means

      a.    men speak grammatically correct language while women's speech is grammatically incorrect.
      b.    linguistic gender differences, such as women using a less forceful style of speaking than men.
      c.    men and women in a society never speak directly to each other after the age of ten.
      d.    language used to describe sexuality is known only to males in some societies.

13.     In Guayaquil, Ecuador, family planning clinics

    a.     were visited by 80 percent of the women who wanted information on birth control methods.

    b.     asked for a large amount of information from the clients while giving them little explanatory information.

    c.     asked for unnecessary monthly visits for examinations and supplies which embarrassed women.

    d.     b and c

    e.     all of the above

14.     Gender ideology

    a.     has sometimes been distorted as the result of research by male ethnographers working with male informants.

    b.     is always more correctly recorded in the work of female ethnographers.

    c.     is more commonly analyzed in research on men's role than in studies of females' roles.

    d.     is no longer a focus of research because of advances in theory since the 1960s.

15.     Women's menstrual fluids

    a.     are polluting in all contexts and in all societies.

    b.     are only polluting in agricultural and industrial societies.

    c.     are polluting only in some contexts while in others they can prevent or even counteract pollution.

    d.     always represent women's impurity in contract with men's purity.

16.     In Lagos, Nigeria, a Yoruba woman

    a.     must defer to her husband but not to any other man.

    b.     while depending on men for security, nevertheless may seek, and frequently gain, power and authority through property ownership.

    c.     must behave as a subordinate in all situations.

    d.     must avoid any expression of interest in the powerful position in the world of economics and politics.

17.   Female infanticide

    a.     does not occur in contemporary societies.
    b.     can involve outright killing, nutritional deprivation, or sex-selective abortion.
    c.     means there is a strong preference for female children.
    d.     means that medical attention is provided for daughters much more frequently than for sons.

18.   It is estimated that the percentage of women who have been physically assaulted by an intimate partner is

    a.     65%.
    b.     28%.
    c.     10%.
    d.     5%.

19.   Human sexuality

    a.     is regulated by all societies.
    b.     usually requires a long period of postpartum sexual abstinence in agricultural societies.
    c.     has been determined to give humans remarkably uniform sex drives across all societies.
    d.     is regulated in a wide variety of ways by all societies, except, that premarital and extramarital sexual relations are always forbidden.

20.   The study of the role of women in agriculture can help address the food crisis in sub-Saharan Africa because

    a.     African women are farmers and extremely important in the food chain.
    b.     African women are not farmers but are extremely important in food processing.
    c.     they hold a high status in their household even though they never supply more than 25 to 30 percent of the labor and management of African food production.
    d.     African woman often have to leave their children with their husband while they go to cities to earn money for the purchase of the family's food.

**TRUE-FALSE**

_____ 1.    Although there is a wide range of variation in gender relations, women are subordinate to men in only horticultural and pastoral societies.

_____ 2.    Purdah is the term for universal female subordination.

_____ 3.    All societies define gender roles in very similar ways.

_____ 4.    Men's roles are always rigidly defined while women's roles are more flexible.

_____ 5.    Abuse by a husband or intimate partner is the most pervasive form of gender-based violence.

_____ 6.    While men entered the work force in greater numbers than women during the present century, women also made significant contributions to factory production in the United States.

_____ 7.    Since the 1950s, occupational segregation in the United States along gender lines has been reduced.

_____ 8.    When women are subordinate to males in their homes they are also subordinate in public.

_____ 9.    Sexual violence, such as rape, is a direct consequence of extreme gender ideology.

_____ 10.    In some societies women's and men's roles overlap considerably.

_____ 11.    All of societies of New Guinea studied by Margaret Mead, define the male gender as subordinate to the female.

_____ 12.    Women entered the textile industry's work force because they were thought to have better manual dexterity than men.

_____ 13.    Using the term "gender" acknowledges that culture plays a part in defining the way members of the two sexes are expected to behave.

_____ 14.    The anthropologist studying family planning clinics in Ecuador recommended that women should be interviewed privately and examined with an awareness of their need for modesty.

____ 15.     All societies of the world define gender alternatives as only female or male.

____ 16.     The feminization of poverty refers to the fact that more than half of all female-headed families in the United States are living in poverty.

____ 17.     Among the Tiwi of North Australia, widowed mothers or sisters could not be manipulated or even coerced by their sons or brothers.

____ 18.     In food collecting societies, the roles performed by men and women are very different but their relative status are similar.

____ 19.     Most programs to improve food production in Africa have been addressed to men because they have mistakenly been thought to have the major responsibility for agricultural production.

____ 20.     In the United States, the percentage of working women with children under the age of six has grown since the last turn of the century.

## SHORT ANSWER

1.   What is the difference between sex and gender?  How can we study the importance of culture in determining gender?

2.   What would be egalitarian gender roles?  What does subordination mean?

3.   What are some of the uniformity's in the way societies divide tasks between women and men?

4.   Which societies are the most are the most highly stratified along gender lines.?  Which are the most egalitarian?

5.    What is gender ideology?  How might male and female informants differ in how they report gender ideology?

6.    Describe the range of variation in cultural regulation of human sexuality.

7.    How does gender definition in the United States compare with that of other societies? Have industrialized societies reduced or eliminated occupational segregation?

8.    Female infanticide is found under what conditions?

9.    What is the relationship of male-biased gender ideology and gender-based violence?

# CHAPTER
## 12
## POLITICAL ORGANIZATION AND SOCIAL CONTROL

## LEARNING OBJECTIVES

Complete the work in this chapter of the Study Guide to improve your understanding of the following objectives. Read them before you begin and after you have finished the definitions and questions. Write a note to yourself about any objective that is still not clear, reread your text's discussion of that topic, and if you continue to have questions, discuss the issue with your classmates and instructor.

Having read and studied Chapter 12, you should be able to:

1.     Define social order and political organization.

2.     Define and identify three dimensions of political organization.

3.     Recognize that all types of political organization have more complex state political systems superimposed over them.

4.     Describe the characteristics of political organization in band societies.

5.     Recognize the significance of pan-tribal associations for tribes and the similarities and differences between tribes and bands.

6.     Understand how the increased social and technological complexity of chiefdoms over bands or tribes is reflected in their political organization.

7.    Define nation and nation-state.

8.    Describe the political organization of state societies and the basis for the authority of the state.

9.    Contrast the four types of political structures discussed by Ferraro in his description of the continuum of variation from acephalous societies to state systems.

10.    Explain three theories that account for the formation of state societies and recognize that independent cases of state formation might require more than one theory for adequate explanation.

11.    Recognize the great importance of informal means of social control for complex state organizations as well as for bands and tribes.

12.    Understand the great diversity in formal means of social control and the significant difference in the objectives of legal systems in more and less complex societies.

## DEFINITIONS AND EXAMPLES

Write out your own definitions and examples from memory.  Compare your answers with those in the book's glossary after defining all of the terms.

Define

1.    power

   _____
   _____
   _____

2.    authority

   _____
   _____
   _____

3.    acephalous society

   _____
   _____
   _____

4.   age grade

_____
_____
_____

5.   ancestor worship

_____
_____
_____

6.   band  society

_____
_____
_____

7.   chiefdom

_____
_____
_____

8.   coercive theory of state formation

_____
_____
_____

9.   corporate lineage

_____
_____
_____

10.   crime

_____
_____
_____

11.   degradation ceremony

_____
_____
_____

12.   deviance

_____
_____
_____

13.   egalitarian

_____
_____
_____

14.   ghost invocation

_____
_____
_____

15.   ghostly vengeance

_____
_____
_____

16.   hydraulic theory of state formation

_____
_____
_____

17.   intermediary

_____
_____
_____

18.   law

_____
_____
_____

19.   Leopard-skin chief

_____
_____
_____

20.    moot

_____

_____

_____

21.    nation

_____

_____

_____

22.    negative sanction

_____

_____

_____

23.    oath

_____

_____

_____

24.    ordeal

_____

_____

_____

25.    pan-tribal mechanism

_____

_____

_____

26.    political coerciveness

_____

_____

_____

27.    political integration

_____

_____

_____

28.   positive sanction

_____

_____

_____

29.   public opinion

_____

_____

_____

30.   rebellion

_____

_____

_____

31.   revolution

_____

_____

_____

32.   segmentary lineage system

_____

_____

_____

33.   song dual

_____

_____

_____

34.   social control

_____

_____

_____

35.   social norm

_____

_____

_____

36.    socialization

_____
_____
_____

37.    specialized political role

_____
_____
_____

38.    state society

_____
_____
_____

39.    tribal society

_____
_____
_____

40.    voluntaristic theory of state formation

_____
_____
_____

41.    witchcraft

_____
_____
_____

## MULTIPLE-CHOICE

1.    Cross-culturally, the political organization of societies

   a.    always involves hierarchy.
   b.    gives most of the political power to a very small group.
   c.    differs in the degree of hierarchy.
   d.    a and b

2.    _____ societies have the least political integration and no permanent leaders.

    a.    State
    b.    Chiefdom
    c.    Tribal
    d.    Band

3.    Intensive agriculture is usually associated with _____ organization.

    a.    state
    b.    chiefdom
    c.    tribal
    d.    band

4.    An example of a band society is the

    a.    Nuer.
    b.    Trobriander.
    c.    !Kung.
    d.    Crow.

5.    Which types of political organization have more complex state political systems superimposed over them?

    a.    bands
    b.    tribes
    c.    chiefdoms
    d.    all of the above

6.    An example of a tribal society is the

    a.    Nuer.
    b.    Trobriander.
    c.    !Kung.
    d.    Hawaiian.

7.    European colonial powers

    a.    altered the nature of traditional chiefs.
    b.    created chiefs in some tribal societies.
    c.    appointed chiefs sometimes held in contempt by their own people as collaborators with repressive and coercive colonial governments.
    d.    all of the above

8.      A segmentary lineage system

   a.    demonstrates the shifting nature of the political structure of tribal societies.
   b.    is less common than tribal organization based on clans.
   c.    is effective in organizing for defense of the entire tribe.
   d.    all of the above

9.      A nation-state

   a.    refers to a group of people who share a common symbolic identity, culture,
         history, and often, religion.
   b.    refers to a particular type of political structure distinct from a band, tribal society,
         or chiefdom.
   c.    refers to a group of people sharing a common cultural background and unified by a
         political structure that they all consider to be legitimate.
   d.    describes clearly almost all societies in the world today.

10.     Until 10,000 years ago, humans lived in

   a.    states.
   b.    tribes.
   c.    chiefdoms.
   d.    bands.

11.     Band societies are most often based on

   a.    foraging.
   b.    horticulture.
   c.    pastoralism.
   d.    intensive agriculture.

12.     Public opinion

   a.    is one of the most compelling reasons for not violating the social norms of a
         society.
   b.    can be influenced by degradation ceremonies.
   c.    has a great deal of importance in many societies.
   d.    all of the above

13.   Individuals who belong to an age set

    a.    only come together as adults to socialize.
    b.    often have shared an intensive period of training in the norms and values of a society.
    c.    are prohibited from socializing with one another.
    d.    always marry one another's sisters.

14.   Members of a corporate lineage group

    a.    always live together.
    b.    never live together.
    c.    often see marriage as an alliance of two lineages, legitimized by bridewealth.
    d.    exert a great deal of social control over but have little economic influence on one another.

15.   Physical punishment

    a.    is seldom found in state societies.
    b.    is seldom found in chiefdoms.
    c.    may legitimately be used by the official authority in state societies.
    d.    is never found in band society.

16.   In cultures with a belief in witchcraft,

    a.    innocent people are often falsely accused and punished for being witches.
    b.    accusations of witchcraft are usually based public opinion, and focus on an individual who has a history of disputes with neighbors or weak kin network.
    c.    accusations are more on the basis of supernatural beliefs than social relations.
    d.    shamans indict witches based on personal antagonisms.

17.   For the Poarch Creek of Alabama to gain federal recognition they

    a.    hired an anthropologist to do necessary research for the group's first petition.
    b.    had to demonstrate that they had maintained a continuous existence as a political unit with viable leadership that had authority over its members.
    c.    had to hide the amount of intermarriage which had occurred with non-Indians.
    d.    could rely totally on the knowledge of their oldest members.

18.    The scholarly research of anthropologists

    a.    never can have much of an impact on the political life of the people they study.
    b.    can have an impact on the political life of the people they study.
    c.    only has an impact on the political life of the people they study if the case study method is used.
    d.    only has an impact on the political life of the people they study if archival data is available for study.

19.    The Customary Law Project in Papua New Guinea

    a.    helped identify and later alleviate certain problems arising from conflicts between customary law and the existing national legal system.
    b.    recorded case studies on only legal disputes between the traditional cultures and the colonial government.
    c.    proved how little value the case study method had for the study of law in non-literate societies.
    d.    created a legal data bank which was completed in 1975.

20.    Complex forms of government developed because

    a.    of the emergence of a tradition of strong chiefs in a single culture of Europe.
    b.    of the emergence of a tradition of strong chiefs in a single culture of Africa.
    c.    of warfare over control of long-range trade.
    d.    for a variety of reasons on which there is relatively little consensus.

## TRUE-FALSE

_____ 1.    State refers to a particular type of political structure and nation refers to a group of people who share a common identity, culture, history, and often religion.

_____ 2.    Before the 1400s, state political organization existed only in Europe.

_____ 3.    States have less labor specialization than any other type of political organization.

_____ 4.    Pan-tribal organizations are the major difference between tribes and bands.

_____ 5.    Corporate lineages seldom exert social control over their members.

_____ 6.      An ordeal is a test to determine the guilt or innocence of an individual.

_____ 7.      In the "ethnographic present" there are no pure bands, tries, or chiefdoms because they all have state political systems superimposed over them.

_____ 8.      The term deviance refers to violation of social norms but what is deviant in one culture may not be deviant in another.

_____ 9.      Some anthropologists only distinguish between acephalous and state societies.

_____ 10.     Where witchcraft is practiced, people reject the idea that crops fail or large numbers of people die because of natural causes.

_____ 11.     Moots are a formal court used to settle domestic disputes in many African societies.

_____ 12.     Positive sanctions include a smile of approval.

_____ 13.     Social norms are behavioral guidelines about what is normal, proper, or expected.

_____ 14.     To say that there are only two types of political structure, state systems and acephalous, is to refer to ideal types.

_____ 15.     Nation-state refers to a group of people sharing a common cultural background even when they do not all consider their political structure to be legitimate.

_____ 16.     Supernatural belief systems may cause people to refrain from antisocial behavior.

_____ 17.     All court systems try to separate the guilty party from society by incarceration.

_____ 18.     Corporal punishment is a type of negative sanction.

_____ 19.     An oath is a formal declaration to some supernatural force that what you are saying is truthful or that you are innocent.

_____ 20.     Serious offenders, in state societies, threaten the very legitimacy of political and legal authority.

## MATCHING

Match the following

a.    band
b.    tribe
c.    chiefdom
d.    state

1.    _____        precolonial Hawaii
2.    _____        !Kung
3.    _____        the United States
4.    _____        colonial Nigeria
5.    _____        Nuer
6.    _____        Hindu India
7.    _____        Muslim Middle East
8.    _____        Eskimo
9.    _____        Masai
10.   _____        colonial Australia

## SHORT ANSWER

1.    What are the concerns of political organization outside of state societies?

2.    What are the three dimensions in which political organizations vary?  What are the four categories of society used in your text?

3.    What are the relationships of complex state political systems to the different types of political organization?  Do band societies' relationships to states different from those of tribal or chiefdom societies?

4.    How are state societies different than other forms of political organization?

5.    What are possible theories for the formation of state societies?  Are any of those adequate explanation for all state societies' origins?

6.    What are important informal means for social control?  What are formal means?

# CHAPTER
## 13
## SOCIAL STRATIFICATION

## LEARNING OBJECTIVES

Complete the work in this chapter of the Study Guide to improve your understanding of the following objectives. Read them before you begin and after you have finished the definitions and questions. Write a note to yourself about any objective that is still not clear, reread your text's discussion of that topic, and if you continue to have questions, discuss the issue with your classmates and instructor.

Having read and studied Chapter 13, you should be able to:

1.      Explain three factors involved in social ranking.

2.      Describe the social and economic organization of egalitarian societies.

3.      Understand how access to power and wealth does not correlate with access to prestige in rank societies.

4.      Recognize the range of socio-economic organization that occurs within stratified societies.

5.      Explain the difference between class and caste societies.

6.      Discuss the contradictions between the ideology and the actual experience of social mobility in the United States.

7.  Understand Ferraro's definitions of race and ethnicity and explain how they are distinct concepts.

8.  Describe the range of ways in which racial and ethnic groups relate to one another.

9.  Discuss the functionalist interpretation of social stratification.

10. Understand the conflict theorist interpretation of stratification as exploitation by the upper levels of hierarchy.

## DEFINITIONS AND EXAMPLES

Write out your own definitions and examples from memory.  Compare your answers with those in the book's glossary after defining all of the terms.

Define

1.  achieved status

    _____
    _____
    _____

2.  ascribed status

    _____
    _____
    _____

3.  assimilation

    _____
    _____
    _____

4.  bourgeoisie

    _____
    _____
    _____

5.  caste

    _____
    _____
    _____

6.    class

_____
_____
_____


7.    conflict theory

_____
_____
_____


8.    egalitarian societies

_____
_____
_____


9.    ethnic group

_____
_____
_____


10.    functional theory

_____
_____
_____


11.    *jati*

_____
_____
_____


12.    nouveau riche

_____
_____
_____


13.    pluralism

_____
_____
_____

14.   population transfer

_____

_____

_____

15.   power

_____

_____

_____

16.   prestige

_____

_____

_____

17.   proletariat

_____

_____

_____

18.   race

_____

_____

_____

19.   rank societies

_____

_____

_____

20.   social mobility

_____

_____

_____

21.   stratified societies

_____

_____

_____

22.    *varnas*

_____

_____

_____


23.    wealth

_____

_____

_____


## MULTIPLE-CHOICE

1.    Wealth, a criterion for measuring social inequality, is

    a.    almost always defined as ownership of manufactured goods.
    b.    culturally defined and varies in form from one society to another.
    c.    enormously variable in the United States and 1 percent of U.S. households control more wealth than the entire bottom 90 percent of households.
    d.    b and c

2.    Power is defined as

    a.    the ability to achieve one's goals and objectives even against the will of others.
    b.    the ability to control wealth.
    c.    the occupation of a position of prestige.
    d.    being esteemed or admired.

3.    Prestige is defined as

    a.    having wealth and respect.
    b.    having power and respect.
    c.    social esteem, respect, or admiration.
    d.    a and b

4.    Inequality of wealth

    a.    is always associated with inequality of power.
    b.    always allows some members of society to force others to do what they order.
    c.    is not associated with inequality of power in all societies.
    d.    a and b

5.   Forcing others to do what you want them to do is a demonstration of

   a.   power.
   b.   wealth.
   c.   prestige.
   d.   b and c

6.   Egalitarian, rank, and stratified are types of societies based on

   a.   levels of social inequality.
   b.   types of religious belief.
   c.   levels of biological evolution.
   d.   types of political organization.

7.   _____ societies have a constantly changing number of high-status positions reflecting the number of qualified candidates.

   a.   Tribal
   b.   Egalitarian
   c.   Rank
   d.   Stratified

8.   In _____ societies the number of high-status positions is limited and usually assigned on the basis of kinship.

   a.   tribal
   b.   egalitarian
   c.   rank
   d.   stratified

9.   Unequal access to rewards is, by and large, inheritable from one generation to another in _____ societies.

   a.   tribal
   b.   egalitarian
   c.   rank
   d.   stratified

10.    Stratified societies developed at approximately

    a.    15,500 B.C.
    b.    10,000 B.C.
    c.    3500 B.C.
    d.    1000 B.C.

11.    A population with similar levels of wealth, prestige, and power is a

    a.    kinship group.
    b.    social class.
    c.    chiefdom.
    d.    state society.

12.    Power in the United States,

    a.    according to our democratic ideology, is in the hands of the people.
    b.    contrary to our democratic ideology, may be concentrated in the hands of a power elite.
    c.    like everywhere else in the world, always overlaps with wealth.
    d.    a and b
    e.    all of the above

13.    Most of the population of the United States is in the

    a.    upper and upper middle classes.
    b.    upper middle and lower middle classes.
    c.    lower middle and working classes.
    d.    working class and working poor.
    e.    underclass

14.    Occupational stratification in the United States

    a.    requires more abstract thinking and less physical labor at the top end.
    b.    has significantly changed since the 1950s.
    c.    is very distinct from the occupational rankings in other parts of the world.
    d.    a and c

15.    The upper class in the United States,

    a.      includes old wealth.
    b.      comprises approximately 4 percent of the population.
    c.      includes top government and judicial officials who have only moderate wealth.
    d.      all of the above

16.    Race is

    a.      different classification systems depending upon what traits are used as the basis for distinguishing groups.
    b.      a division of humans into Mongoloid, Caucasoid, and Negroid.
    c.      scientifically significant physical differences in contemporary human populations.
    d.      determined by physical characteristics.

17.    As a scientific concept, race

    a.      is not terribly significant.
    b.      has no validly in determines political structures.
    c.      does not recognize that a continuum of human physical types have resulted from the interbreeding of humans.
    d.      all of the above

18.    Ethnic groups

    a.      are interbreeding populations whose members share a greater number of traits with one another than they do with people outside the group.
    b.      perceive themselves as sharing cultural traits passed on from generation to generation.
    c.      are the politically correct way to refer to racial groups.
    d.      a and c

19.    Research on diabetic Hispanic patients in Texas

    a.      found that they, unlike members of other ethnic groups, often fail to follow through on recommended treatment behaviors.
    b.      found that they had a particularly high rate of noncompliance with prescribed treatment behaviors.
    c.      they  adapted their self-care behavior to the social realities of their everyday lives, especially their limited financial resources and their desire to conduct "normal" social relationships.
    d.      b and c

20.    Groups with different access to wealth, power, and prestige in Camden, New Jersey

    a.    were able to express their desires for the rehabilitation of Farnham Park.
    b.    were able to prevent the area's neighbors from using Farnham Park.
    c.    restored Farnham Park so that it was primarily a place suitable for young children.
    d.    rid Farnham Park of the presence of unemployed youth and teenagers who "hung out."

## TRUE-FALSE

_____ 1.    The underclass in the United States are the working poor.

_____ 2.    Stratified societies may have either open class or rigid caste structure.

_____ 3.    Ascribed status is based on hard work and a high education level.

_____ 4.    Population transfer, a negative relationship of interracial or interethnic groups, includes the relocation of 16,000 Cherokee from North Carolina to Oklahoma and the relocation of Japanese-Americans during World War II.

_____ 5.    Assimilation means two or more groups living in harmony by retaining their own racial or ethnic heritage, pride, and identity.

_____ 6.    According to some social scientists, the owners and managers of major corporations, advisors to governments, and members of commissions and agencies have concentrated power in the United States.

_____ 7.    Achieved status comes from positions that an individual can choose, or at least have some control over.

_____ 8.    Endogamy maintains caste social boundaries.

_____ 9.    The upper class in the United States comprises approximately four percent of the population.

_____ 10.    In rank societies, high-prestige positions are usually based on kinship.

_____ 11.    The functionalist theory of social inequality implies that social stratification should be maintained because it ensures that the best qualified people fill the top positions.

_____ 12.    Most people in the United States remain in the social class into which they are born.

_____ 13.   Physical traits used in some systems of racial classification are inherited independently of other traits used by other such systems.

_____ 14.   Pluralism is when two or more ethnic groups live together in harmony while retaining their own ethnic heritage, pride, and identity.

_____ 15.   Conflict theorists argue that social inequality should be minimized or eliminated.

_____ 16.   Egalitarian societies are often transformed when they come into contact with state societies.

_____ 17.   Unlike most other class societies, the United States has fluid movement of people among its social classes.

_____ 18.   Extermination of one ethnic group by another occurred under Hitler, in the former Yugoslavia, and in Rwanda.

_____ 19.   Hispanic diabetic patients found it very difficult to cook food for their families that they themselves were not allowed to eat.

_____ 20.   Some human societies have had no clear-cut division of society into hierarchically ranked strata.

## SHORT ANSWER

1.   Explain how the three dimensions of social inequality are both interrelated and can operate independently.

2.   How do the three types of societies based on levels of social inequality differ from one another?

3.   Describe the social and economic organization of egalitarian societies. What are their basic differences from stratified societies?

4.    What is the difference between caste and class societies?  How much social and or economic mobility is found in either?

5.    What is race?  How are people classified by race?

6.    What is ethnicity?  What does ethnicity have to do with conflict in some societies?

7.    How is the United States a melting pot?  How is it not?

8.    Describe the six ways in which racial and ethnic groups may live together.

9.    What is the functionalist interpretation of stratification?  What are its weaknesses?

10.    What is the conflict theory of stratification?  What are its weaknesses?

# CHAPTER
# 14
# RELIGION

## LEARNING OBJECTIVES

Complete the work in this chapter of the Study Guide to improve your understanding of the following objectives. Read them before you begin and after you have finished the definitions and questions. Write a note to yourself about any objective that is still not clear, reread your text's discussion of that topic, and if you continue to have questions, discuss the issue with your classmates and instructor.

Having read and studied Chapter 14, you should be able to:

1.  Define and critically evaluate the concept of religion.

2.  Explain the focus of anthropological interest in the functions of religion and acknowledge that anthropologists are not interested in proving which religion is the best.

3.  Distinguish between religion and magic.

4.  Explain the difference between sorcery and witchcraft.

5.  Describe what myths are and what they do.

6.  Understand the social and the psychological functions of religion.

7.  Describe Wallace's four categories of religious organization.

8.    Give an example of an individualistic cult.

9.    Explain the difference between shamanistic cults and communal cults.

10.    Evaluate the relationship between ecclesiastical cults and state societies.

11.    Describe how religion can play an important role in transforming a society.

12.    Give examples and describe the functions of revitalization cults.

## DEFINITIONS AND EXAMPLES

Write out your own definitions and examples from memory.  Compare your answers with those in the book's glossary after defining all of the terms.

Define

1.    religion

_____

_____

_____

2.    cargo cults

_____

_____

_____

3.    communal cults

_____

_____

_____

4.    ecclesiastical cults

_____

_____

_____

5.    economic behavior

_____

_____

_____

6.     individualistic cults

_____

_____

_____

7.     kinship behavior

_____

_____

_____

8.     liberation theology

_____

_____

_____

9.     magic

_____

_____

_____

10.    mahdist movement

_____

_____

_____

11.    millenarian movement

_____

_____

_____

12.    nativistic movement

_____

_____

_____

13.    psychological functions of religion

_____

_____

_____

14.    religious behavior

_____

_____

_____

15.    religious nationalism

_____

_____

_____

16.    revitalization movement

_____

_____

_____

17.    rite of passage

_____

_____

_____

18.    rite of solidarity

_____

_____

_____

19.    separatist Christian church

_____

_____

_____

20.    shaman

_____

_____

_____

21.    shamanistic cults

_____

_____

_____

22.    social functions of religion

_____
_____
_____

23.    sorcery

_____
_____
_____

24.    supernatural beliefs

_____
_____
_____

25.    vision quest

_____
_____
_____

26.    witchcraft

_____
_____
_____


## MULTIPLE-CHOICE

1.    Religion is

   a.    patterned behaviors.
   b.    a set of beliefs.
   c.    beliefs concerning supernatural beings and forces.
   d.    all of the above

2.    Religion is

   a.    a universal, found in all cultures.
   b.    a cultural phenomenon rather than an individual one.
   c.    an individual phenomenon rather than a cultural one.
   d.    a and b

3.    A nonrational system of belief is

    a.    mathematics.
    b.    religion.
    c.    magic.
    d.    all of the above
    e.    b and c

4.    Sorcery is

    a.    involuntary.
    b.    unconscious.
    c.    the deliberate use of supernatural powers to bring about harm.
    d.    the same thing as witchcraft.

5.    Religions and magic are

    a.    rational.
    b.    irrational.
    c.    ways of dealing with the major issues of human existence.
    d.    a and c

6.    The _____ function of religion involves the creation of powerful social bonds through which people share religious beliefs, practices, and rituals.

    a.    psychological
    b.    emotional
    c.    sociological
    d.    economic

7.    Providing answers based upon supernatural authority is part of the _____ function of religion.

    a.    cognitive
    b.    emotional
    c.    sociological
    d.    economic

8.      The separatist churches in South Africa

        a.      increased the conflict in South Africa.
        b.      created resentment of the white power structure.
        c.      may have blinded the members of the Black Christian churches to the exploitation
                of the apartheid government.
        d.      a and b

9.      Ecclesiastic cults

        a.      have full-time religious specialists.
        b.      are an individualistic form of religion.
        c.      perform rites for the community.
        d.      a and c

10.     Rituals with stages of separation, transition, and incorporation are called rites of

        a.      solidarity.
        b.      passage.
        c.      trial.
        d.      corporation.

11.     Rituals directed toward the welfare of the entire community are called rites of

        a.      solidarity.
        b.      passage.
        c.      trial.
        d.      corporation.

12.     Witchcraft

        a.      is only found in small-scale societies in the nonwestern world.
        b.      is found in  highly industrialized parts of the world including the United State,
                Canada, and Western European countries.
        c.      does not make a distinction between magic used for beneficial and those used for
                malevolent purposes.
        d.      a and c

13.    Religious nationalism

    a.    calls for a fundamentalist religious state that does not tolerate nonbelievers.
    b.    is found only in Muslim countries.
    c.    has no supporters in the United States.
    d.    is found only in the Middle East.

14.    The ruling class usually supplies the priests of

    a.    shamanistic cults.
    b.    ecclesiastic cults.
    c.    ancestral cults.
    d.    modern cults.

15.    Revitalization movements have occurred in

    a.    colonial North America.
    b.    sixteenth-century Europe.
    c.    contemporary America.
    d.    Africa.
    e.    all of the above

16.    Hostetler, the anthropologist that worked with the Amish found that

    a.    Amish teenagers would greatly benefit from attending public high schools.
    b.    Amish teenagers would suffer great psychological harm if forced to attend public high schools.
    c.    the Amish were a cult.
    d.    Amish teenagers should be the ones to choose what high school they would attend.

17.    Filipino Americans

    a.    have little understanding of Western medical care.
    b.    never believe that illness is caused by supernatural factors such as sorcerers, witches, and ancestral spirits.
    c.    have beneficial or neutral folk practices which can be built into health care strategies in order to establish rapport with patients.
    d.    b and c

18.    Handsome Lake, a Seneca Indian in New York State in the 1800s,

    a.    founded a new religion because of the economic and social progress they experienced through their relationship with the Federal government.
    b.    urged changes in agricultural practices and social organization.
    c.    developed a religion which called for changed morals but not changed behavior.
    d.    fought to maintain the traditional importance of the matrilineage.

19.    There are no religious specialists in

    a.    ecclesiastical cults.
    b.    communal cults.
    c.    individualistic cults.
    d.    shamanistic cults.

20.    Religion, as a conservative force within a society, supports the status quo

    a.    by keeping people in line through supernatural sanctions.
    b.    relieving social conflict.
    c.    providing explanations for unfortunate events.
    d.    all of the above

## TRUE-FALSE

_____ 1.    Anthropologists' research identifies the various religious beliefs in the world, how they function, to what extent they are held, and how much they affect human behavior.

_____ 2.    In North American cities most religious practitioners are women.

_____ 3.    Most revitalization movements end the domination of oppressive forces.

_____ 4.    In ecclesiastical cults there is a hierarchy of full-time professional clergy.

_____ 5.    Interest in Satanism has been considerably reduced with the increase of modern industrialization in contemporary societies.

_____ 6.    The individualistic cult is the most basic level of religious organization and usually associated with food-collecting societies.

_____ 7.    Religion almost never diffuses the anger and hostility of disenfranchised people in stratified societies.

_____ 8.     In all societies shamen take hallucinogenic drugs to achieve an altered state of consciousness.

_____ 9.     Ecclesiastical cults includes Hinduism, Buddhism, Christianity, Judaism, and Islam.

_____ 10.    Ecclesiastical cults include the religions of the Aztecs, Incas, ancient Greeks, and ancient Egyptians.

_____ 11.    Rites of passage celebrate the transition of a person from one social status to another.

_____ 12.    Witchcraft is inborn and generally involuntary.

_____ 13.    Magic is a direct attempt to control and manipulate supernatural forces.

_____ 14.    Church membership in the United States has grown, not declined, steadily over the last several hundred years.

_____ 15.    Liberation theology used Catholic beliefs to maintain the status quo in Latin American counties in the 1970s.

_____ 16.    Mahdist movements in the Muslim world are revitalization movements.

_____ 17.    In ecclesiastic cults rituals are conducted a regular intervals by full-time priests.

_____ 18.    Religious nationalism combines fundamentalist religious orthodoxy with contemporary political institutions.

_____ 19.    Christianity predominates in the Americas, Europe, and Asia.

_____ 20.    Kikuyu initiation, a rite of passage, involves a physical operation.

## MATCHING

Match the following

a.      individualistic cult
b.      ecclesiastic cult
c.      communal cult
d.      shamanistic cult

1.      _____ stratified societies
2.      _____ food collecting societies
3.      _____ full-time priests
4.      _____ part-time shaman
5.      _____ female shaman
6.      _____ male priests
7.      _____ the United States
8.      _____ the Crow vision quest
9.      _____ "possessed" healers
10.     _____ rites of solidarity

## SHORT ANSWER

1.      Why does the definition of supernatural influence the definition of religion?  Why is religion said to be universal?


2.      How is religion different from magic and sorcery?


3.      What are the social and psychological functions of religion?  Give an example of each from North American culture.

4.    How do Wallace's four categories of religious organizations differ?

5.    How do religions maintain the status quo in societies today?  How do they foster change?

# CHAPTER
## 15
## ART

## LEARNING OBJECTIVES

Complete the work in this chapter of the Study Guide to improve your understanding of the following objectives. Read them before you begin and after you have finished the definitions and questions. Write a note to yourself about any objective that is still not clear, reread your text's discussion of that topic, and if you continue to have questions, discuss the issue with your classmates and instructor.

Having read and studied Chapter 15, you should be able to:

1.  Give a clear definition of art while recognizing that art is integrated into the whole of culture.

2.  Explain why such activities as carving, weaving, or telling folktales can be art.

3.  Describe the significance of both process and product for the definition of art.

4.  Understand the forms of art most common in nomadic or semi-nomadic societies and how they differ from those of complex societies.

5.  Recognize the psychological functions of art for the artist as well as for the audience.

6.  Describe the contribution of art to the social integration of a society.

7.  Recognize how distinct the creation of art is across cultures.

8.   Explain the ways in which art can preserve the status quo of a society both symbolically and mechanically.

9.   Understand the importance of culture in determining what a person actually hears in music.

10.  Explain how dance and verbal arts can be integral aspects of socialization.

## DEFINITIONS AND EXAMPLES

Write out your own definitions and examples from memory.  Compare your answers with those in the book's glossary after defining all of the terms.

Define

1.   art

_____
_____
_____

2.   dance

_____
_____
_____

3.   ethnomusicology

_____
_____
_____

4.   folklore

_____
_____
_____

5.   folktales

_____
_____
_____

6.    graphic arts

_____

_____

_____

7.    *hija*

_____

_____

_____

8.    legends

_____

_____

_____

9.    music

_____

_____

_____

10.    myths

_____

_____

_____

11.    plastic arts

_____

_____

_____

12.    primitive art

_____

_____

_____

13.    transformational

_____

_____

_____

**MULTIPLE-CHOICE**

1.    Anthropologists are interested in

    a.    process, products, and transformations of forms.
    b.    the emotional responses of a population to art.
    c.    aesthetic responses of members of society.
    d.    all of the above
    e.    a and c

2.    Artistic expression, according to anthropologists,

    a.    is either primitive or techno-industrial.
    b.    must have an international appeal and market.
    c.    can include dance, pottery, and cloth.
    d.    must evoke a universal emotional response.

3.    Anthropologists argue that it is ethnocentric to use the term

    a.    folklore.
    b.    primitive.
    c.    legend.
    d.    myth.

4.    Emotional responses to art

    a.    only occur in state societies with significant leisure time.
    b.    occur only in very complex and very simple societies, not in the more practical horticultural and pastoral societies.
    c.    may be both positive and negative:  that is, art may make people feel good or it may make them feel bad or angry.
    d.    a and c

5.    Artistic standards are

    a.    uniform across cultures.
    b.    uniform within a society.
    c.    usually set by members of the upper classes in stratified societies.
    d.    usually set by the artistic community in stratified societies.

6.    Artistic expression includes

    a.    Eskimo body tattooing.
    b.    the Japanese tea ceremony.
    c.    Nubian body decoration.
    d.    all of the above
    e.    b and c

7.    Art, in small-scale societies, is

    a.    more often embedded in other aspects of the culture than in complex societies.
    b.    often more democratic than in complex societies.
    c.    almost always created on rock walls or cliffs.
    d.    a and b

8.    Artistic expression functions

    a.    as an artist's release of emotional energy in a very concrete or visible way.
    b.    to evoke only pleasurable emotional responses in audiences.
    c.    to always sustain the longevity of a society.
    d.    occurs in egalitarian societies.

9.    Graphic and plastic arts include

    a.    weaving.
    b.    architecture.
    c.    dance.
    d.    all of the above
    e.    a and b

10.   Anthropologists who study dance are interested in

    a.    its artistic process.
    b.    its cultural context.
    c.    the social relations influenced by performance.
    d.    all of the above

11.   In South America,

    a.    arpilleristas opposed the status quo under Pinochet.
    b.    arpilleristas supported the status quo under Pinochet.
    c.    liberation theater opposed the status quo.
    d.    a and c

12.    Folklore includes

    a.    toasts.
    b.    folk medicine.
    c.    epitaphs.
    d.    all of the above

13.    Myths

    a.    include all types of narratives.
    b.    focus on the small details of daily life.
    c.    involve supernatural beings.
    d.    b and c

14.    Folktales

    a.    focus on the big issues of life.
    b.    have no particular basis in history.
    c.    are more secular than myths.
    d.    b and c

15.    In all cultures, artistic endeavors

    a.    take priority over survival needs.
    b.    are only carried out when a surplus of food is stored.
    c.    reflect the human need to express self.
    d.    are usually limited to a small group of artistic specialists.

16.    *Hija,* an archaic rhetorical art form,

    a.    uses a vocabulary not understood by much of the population.
    b.    was based on the assumption that warriors could acquire supernatural power by insulting their opponents in verse.
    c.    was used by Iraq and Saudi television and the Kuwaiti television in exile.
    d.    all of the above

17.    The kayaks made by the Aleutians

    a.    were strong but not capable of the fast speed of modern kayaks.
    b.    were artistic creations with a very simple technology.
    c.    had an important structural advantage over modern boats, the flexible bearings for the joints of the wood frame.
    d.    all of the above

18.    The popularity of Luke Skywalker and Obi-Wan Kenobi indicate that

   a.    mythology has significance for the West even though it no longer is part of nonwestern cultures.
   b.    even the West has mythology.
   c.    mythology has no lessons for life in complex societies.
   d.    the West has out-grown mythology.

19.    Liberation theater

   a.    involved oppressed people from local communities.
   b.    trained oppressed people to assume protagonist roles, offer solutions to oppressive scenarios, and discuss strategies for change.
   c.    was seen as a rehearsal for the revolution, not the revolution itself.
   d.    all of the above

20.    Art usually contributes to the *status quo* when it

   a.    is created by the working class of a contemporary societies.
   b.    is created by a minority population.
   c.    has a religious base.
   d.    a and b

## TRUE-FALSE

_____ 1.    Definitions of art differ with the purposes of the definers but all conclude that art is a process, not a product.

_____ 2.    Art is a creative process which produces an emotional response.

_____ 3.    Art usually conveys a message and is produced with a certain level of skill.

_____ 4.    The focus of anthropologists who study art is on primitive art.

_____ 5.    Aesthetically meaningful forms and processes are found in all societies.

_____ 6.    Navajo sand painting which is as much religion, myth, and healing as it is art, demonstrates the embeddedness of small-scale societies' art in other aspects of the culture.

_____ 7.    Art can reinforce social bonds and cultural themes but almost never acts as a mechanism of social control.

_____ 8.        Ethnomusicology is the cross-cultural study of music.

_____ 9.        Solo singing is a characteristic of both small-scale and stratified societies.

_____ 10.       Dance can express political values and attitudes.

_____ 11.       Folktales are always recognized as the work of a specific artist but cannot be analyzed in terms of plot, character development, and structure.

_____ 12.       Myths are artistic expressions rather than explanations of the really big issues of human existence.

_____ 13.       The Yanomamo myths of creation create strong sanctions in the society against violence and sexuality.

_____ 14.       Folklore is difficult to define precisely but generally refers to unwritten verbal arts.

_____ 15.       Legends are specific types of narratives that involve supernatural beings and explain the major issues of human existence.

_____ 16.       Bert and Ernie of Sesame Street are examples of a form of art that educates children.

_____ 17.       The Eskimo artist today produces a craft rather than art.

_____ 18.       Standard setters are often members of the elite and art is often owned and controlled by the upper classes in North America today.

_____ 19.       Masks thought to embody spirits have been used for social control, especially in the administration of justice.

_____ 20.       In state societies only the members of the upper class have the knowledge, skill, and ability to produce art.

## SHORT ANSWER

1.      Explain how art is a process not only products.  How does the idea of art as a process influence our definition?

2.    Describe the variety of forms art takes cross-culturally.  Why do anthropologist not use
      the term primitive in reference to art?

3.    When does art support the status quo?  When does it challenge it?

4.    When are artists specialists?

5.    What are the major differences between art in small-scale and complex societies?

# CHAPTER
# 16
# CULTURE CHANGE

## LEARNING OBJECTIVES

Complete the work in this chapter of the Study Guide to improve your understanding of the following objectives. Read them before you begin and after you have finished the definitions and questions. Write a note to yourself about any objective that is still not clear, reread your text's discussion of that topic, and if you continue to have questions, discuss the issue with your classmates and instructor.

Having read and studied Chapter 16, you should be able to:

1.    Understand how change is essential to all cultures.

2.    Describe the two processes that cause cultures to change internally.

3.    Explain the difference between invention and innovation and recognize the greater impact of the latter.

4.    Recognize that diffusion is a two-way process and understand what is involved in the selection of characteristics that are diffused.

5.    Explain how acculturation is distinct from diffusion.

6.    Describe why change in one part of a culture is likely to bring about changes in other parts.

7.    Explain three reasons why a society might resist cultural change.

8.    Describe the process of urbanization.

9.    Explain why the dichotomous rural-urban model is simplistic and the concept of circulation of labor is more realistic.

10.    Explain occupational duality.

11.    Understand the variety of processes involved in urban migration.

12.    Describe the stratification of economic development.

13.    Understand the contrast between modernization and world system theory.

14.    Explain the role of multinational corporations in economic development and the process of neocolonialism.

## DEFINITIONS AND EXAMPLES

Write out your own definitions and examples from memory.  Compare your answers with those in the book's glossary after defining all of the terms.

Define

1.    acculturation

_____
_____
_____


2.    circulation of labor

_____
_____
_____


3.    Conference of Berlin

_____
_____
_____

4.    cultural boundary maintenance

_____
_____
_____

5.    diffusion

_____
_____
_____

6.    innovation

_____
_____
_____

7.    invention

_____
_____
_____

8.    kwashiorkor

_____
_____
_____

9.    less-developed countries (LDCs)

_____
_____
_____

10.    linked change

_____
_____
_____

11.    marginal people

_____
_____
_____

12.   modernization

_____

_____

_____

13.   modernization theory

_____

_____

_____

14.   multinational corporations

_____

_____

_____

15.   neocolonialism

_____

_____

_____

16.   occupational duality

_____

_____

_____

17.   urbanization

_____

_____

_____

18.   voluntary associations

_____

_____

_____

19.   world systems theory

_____

_____

_____

**MULTIPLE-CHOICE**

1.    An external mechanism which changes culture is

      a.    innovation.
      b.    invention.
      c.    diffusion.
      d.    all of the above

2.    The idea that unintentional change, over the long run, has a greater impact on cultures than intentional invention, was argued by

      a.    Ralph Linton.
      b.    Levi-Strauss.
      c.    Radcliffe-Brown.
      d.    Emile Durkheim.

3.    Inventions usually

      a.    develop because there is a pressing need.
      b.    are very financially beneficial.
      c.    are not recognized when they are unconscious or accidental even through they may make a significant cumulative contribution.
      d.    a and b

4.    Diffusion plays a prominent role in cultural change because it

      a.    is a one-way process which speeds up the progress of the human race.
      b.    advances the societies with the most original cultures beyond those that have adopted the ideas and practices of others.
      c.    allows humans to pool their creative resources and rapidly develop.
      d.    was important in historical times even though it is less important than inventions today.

5.    Because only a small number of cultural elements are diffused from one culture to another,

      a.    diffusion is less important than invention for culture change.
      b.    contemporary societies have very little influence on one another.
      c.    contemporary societies have a very limited capacity to understand one another.
      d.    there are significant cultural differences in the contemporary world.

6.    The pizza

    a.    was invented in North America.
    b.    diffused from Italy to the United States in the late nineteenth century.
    c.    has been modified to include materials not used in Italy.
    d.    b and c

7.    As a part of culture, technology is

    a.    less likely to change than behavior.
    b.    less likely to change than ideas.
    c.    especially resistant to change.
    d.    more likely to change than ideas or behavior patterns.

8.    Linked changes

    a.    are similar changes in two distinct cultures.
    b.    no longer occur because of the advent of modern communication and transportation systems.
    c.    may have a significant impact of public life but seldom influence family life.
    d.    are changes in other parts of a culture following a change in one part.

9.    The forced borrowing from a dominant culture under conditions of external pressure is

    a.    innovation.
    b.    acculturation.
    c.    centralization.
    d.    displacement.

10.    If a society forbids the use of other languages it

    a.    must be the dominant political force in the world.
    b.    may be using its own language to remain culturally separate from other groups.
    c.    must be primitive.
    d.    may be trying to facilitate the process of diffusion.

11.    To maintain cultural boundaries, a society

    a.    must be geographically isolated.
    b.    must have no political ties with other societies.
    c.    strengthens and glorifies its own traditions and discourages borrowing from other cultures.
    d.    must have no social ties with other societies.

12.    When people in a society understand the likely outcome of the project and recognize that it would bring about undesired changes they are likely to resist

    a.    development projects.
    b.    Peace Corp projects.
    c.    missionary projects.
    d.    all of the above

13.    People resist changes in their culture because

    a.    they don't usually comprehend the advantages of the change.
    b.    the proposed change is not compatible with the existing value system.
    c.    quality may be more important than quantity.
    d.    all of the above
    e.    b and c

14.    The rural-urban dichotomy suggests that

    a.    cities are more progressive and secular than rural areas.
    b.    rural areas are more economically interdependent than urban centers.
    c.    country dwellers are more impersonal and blasé that residents of cities.
    d.    all of the above

15.    The circulation of labor

    a.    describes permanent rural migration to cities.
    b.    describes permanent return migration from cities to rural areas  .
    c.    recognizes that migrants may move back and forth between rural and urban areas.
    d.    changes rural communities of origin even though most urban host communities experience little change because of rural migration.

16.    Family members

    a.    in rural areas depend on urban wage earners for economic assistance.
    b.    in rural areas depend on urban wage earners help in finding jobs in the city.
    c.    can be seen as members of one family with both a rural and urban households.
    d.    all of the above

17.    Voluntary associations

    a.    serve only economic functions.
    b.    may serve social as well as economic functions.
    c.    provide an individual with a sense of belonging even if they are marginal to city life.
    d.    b and c

18.    Anthropological research on the impact of a part of the U.S. interstate highway system on a residential neighborhood in Charlotte, North Carolina, found that the

    a.    highway construction was having serious negative consequences on the residents.
    b.    government wanted to relocate most of the residents because of the road construction.
    c.    state wanted evidence that the new highway was bringing more opportunities to the neighborhood.
    d.    required impact study was a waste of government funds.

19.    World System Theory

    a.    is based on the traditional-versus-modern dichotomy.
    b.    describes the rich and poor nations of the world are fundamentally different because of innate culture features.
    c.    explains that the wealthy countries of the world achieved high levels of development by exploiting other regions.
    d.    explains that the wealthy countries of the world took the natural resources of other regions leaving their people and markets untouched.

20.    The USAID funded research project in Swaziland on the impact of changing patterns of marriage on fertility found that

    a.    the more educated a woman, the more likely she was to have a smaller family.
    b.    the more educated a woman, the more likely she was to have a large but healthy family.
    c.    women were marrying on an average of five years younger than they had in the past.
    d.    women were waiting until they were in their thirties to marry.

**TRUE-FALSE**

_____ 1.    Many of the benefits of economic development have been either illusory or downright detrimental.

_____ 2.    Cultural change almost always creates improved ways of living for people.

_____ 3.    When people develop more cash crops their diets usually improve.

_____ 4.    All cultures change to some degree over time.

_____ 5.    Many of more "modern" lifestyles result in a marked increase in diseases associated with the industrialized world.

_____ 6.    Multinational corporations almost always directly exploit LDCs.

_____ 7.    Neocolonialism is a process where the wealthy former colonial nations continue to exercise considerable political, economic, and military power over the less-developed nations.

_____ 8.    Modern people believe that given sufficient time, energy, and money, there is little or nothing that can escape their control or cannot be changed.

_____ 9.    The modern world is very stratified in terms of economic development, life expectancy, and infant mortality.

_____ 10.   Modernization theory is very distinct form the "culture of poverty" which blames poverty on the poor.

_____ 11.   Resistance to the efforts of foreigners to bring about change in a society is solely based on ignorance.

_____ 12.   For South American Indians flexibility in a work schedule may be more important than high wages.

_____ 13.   No more than ten percent of the items in any culture, including our own, originated in that culture.

_____ 14.   Food taboos can set cultures apart from one another.

_____ 15.   Kente cloth, Mao jackets, and black leather jackets can all be expressions of cultural uniqueness depending upon who is wearing the clothing.

_____ 16.    Traditional Lapp culture has always placed considerable emphasis on transportation systems and mobility.

_____ 17.    The percentage of people living in cities in the industrialized world is leveling off, and the most dramatic rates of urbanization in recent years are found in the less-developed countries.

_____ 18.    According to Durkheim rural societies are held together by "mechanical solidarity" and urban, complex societies by "organic solidarity."

_____ 19.    Occupational duality is managing both cash crop farming a rural area and wage employment in the city.

_____ 20.    It is possible to be an innovator without being an inventor.

## SHORT ANSWER

1.    What is the relationship of ethnography to change in human cultures?

2.    Compare the importance of invention and innovation on culture.  What kind of people become inventors or innovators?

3.    Describe the process of diffusion.

4.    Describe the relative importance of innovation and diffusion for cultural change?

5.    How is acculturation different from other types of diffusion?

6.      What forces oppose cultural change?


7.      How had the rate of urbanization changed over time?  What problems does it create?


8.      What is the relationship of rural and urban areas?  What is wrong the dichotomous rural-urban model?  Explain the concept of the circulation of labor.


9.      What is modernization theory?  What are its limitations?


10.     What is world system theory?  What are its limitations?

# CHAPTER
## 17
## THE FUTURE OF ANTHROPOLOGY

## LEARNING OBJECTIVES

Complete the work in this chapter of the Study Guide to improve your understanding of the following objectives. Read them before you begin and after you have finished the definitions and questions. Write a note to yourself about any objective that is still not clear, reread your text's discussion of that topic, and if you continue to have questions, discuss the issue with your classmates and instructor.

Having read and studied Chapter 17, you should be able to:

1. Distinguish between the traditional aim of documenting cultures of isolated people and the contemporary anthropological approach.

2. Understand why anthropologists argue that the contemporary world is not a melting pot.

3. Describe anthropological concern with the survival of indigenous peoples.

4. Explain how anthropologists can validly study complex societies.

5. Understand what is meant by the term, "culture broker" and explain what it means to say that culture brokers make anthropological data available to nonanthropologists.

## DEFINITIONS AND EXAMPLES

Write out your own definitions and examples from memory.  Compare your answers with those in the book's glossary after defining all of the terms.

Define

1.    cultural broker

_____
_____
_____

2.    human rights

_____
_____
_____

3.    indigenous peoples

_____
_____
_____

4.    Massacre at Parallel Eleven

_____
_____
_____

## MULTIPLE-CHOICE

1.    The pace at which cultures change

    a.    remains the same although it seems to speed up as one ages.
    b.    can seem overwhelming, creating future shock.
    c.    has accelerated in recent decades.
    d.    b and c
    e.    all the above

2.    Cultures untouched by the modern world

    a.    have never existed.
    b.    will not be the focus of future anthropological research.
    c.    will disappear into the single global culture that is forming.
    d.    have never been a traditional focus of anthropological research.

3.      When we say the world is getting smaller we

   a.      are displaying our ignorance about geography.
   b.      are stating that reliable data on other cultures is universally available.
   c.      mean that the earth is actually shrinking physically.
   d.      mean that because of advances in transportation and communication it is now
           easier to have contact with other parts of the globe.

4.      The future of cultural anthropology is

   a.      bleak because of cultural change.
   b.      limited because it is just a matter of years before all cultures become a single one.
   c.      not limited because there will continue to be cultural diversity.
   d.      in basic rather than applied research.

5.       In the future, anthropology will place emphasis on

   a.      the study of complex societies such as our own.
   b.      the survival of indigenous peoples.
   c.      greater involvement with developing solutions for societal problems.
   d.      all of the above.

6.      Indigenous people

   a.      do not, as a group, control the national government of the countries within which
           they live.
   b.      are descendants of the earliest populations that survive in the area.
   c.      live in societies isolated from industrialized countries.
   d.      all of the above
   e.      a and b

7.      Indigenous people in Brazil

   a.      have been totally modernized by contact with urban populations.
   b.      are an example of the degradation of native people through violent attacks and
           introduced disease.
   c.      have been isolated from the encroaching gold miners by a government plan which
           protects them.
   d.      have been entirely exterminated through genocide.

8.    Cultural Survival, Inc., a nonprofit organization,

    a.    sponsors only academic research on the last days of indigenous peoples.
    b.    supports projects designed to help indigenous peoples survive the changes brought about by contact with industrial societies.
    c.    supports economic projects that are run by the people themselves.
    d.    b and c

9.    In recent years, anthropologists have studied

    a.    retirement communities.
    b.    adaptive strategies of urban tramps.
    c.    hippie lifestyles.
    d.    all of the above
    e.    a and c

10.    Anthropologists working in their own complex societies,

    a.    face only problems similar to those found in any field site.
    b.    have a sensitivity to ethnic diversity.
    c.    run the risk of prejudice because they lack the outsider perspective.
    d.    all of the above
    e.    b and c

11.    Anthropological study of U.S. society has explored

    a.    railroad engineers as an occupational subculture.
    b.    construction workers as an occupational subculture.
    c.    football and food as popular culture.
    d.    all of the above
    e.    a and c

12.    To increase the use of anthropological research by policymakers, anthropologists must

    a.    take more time to carry out thorough research.
    b.    be clear about possible sources of resistance to using the findings.
    c.    insist on keeping their research distinct from that of nonanthropologists.
    d.    keep their research goals hidden from their sponsors.

13.    People working in other cultures today

a.    often are ignorant of previously gathered anthropological data that could facilitate the work they are attempting.
b.    always find themselves in situations for which there is no previous anthropological research that can improve their understanding of another culture.
c.    have vast amounts of readily accessible and easily understood cultural data.
d.    have little need for the results of anthropological research on other ways of life.

14.    Anthropologists must

a.    translate their research findings into terms that can be used by nonanthropologists.
b.    train others to become cultural brokers.
c.    become cultural brokers.
d.    all of the above
e.    b and c

15.    Anthropology involves the

a.    study of only primitive tribes.
b.    study of only food collectors, horticulturalists, and pastoralists.
c.    comparative study of cultures.
d.    study of primitive tribes and traditional cultures.

16.    The Industrial Revolution in Europe

a.    led to expansion of population and consumerism only in Europe and North America.
b.    led people of the industrializing world to gain control of and exploit natural resources wherever they might be.
c.    had no impact of the indigenous peoples of the world.
d.    a and c

17.    Natural resources found in Asia and Africa were

a.    a major motivation for the colonization of the nonwestern world.
b.    so isolated as to be economically unattractive to European industries.
c.    a major motivation which gave Europeans an awareness of the rights of indigenous populations.
d.    acquired by Europeans without taking land from the indigenous populations.

18.    Indigenous peoples in Brazil

    a.    have been exposed to diseases through the roadbuilding of the government.
    b.    control most of the gold mining in the area.
    c.    are adequately protected by the government from outsiders invading their territory.
    d.    have experienced economic exploitation but not had their lives threatened.

## TRUE-FALSE

____ 1.    The chances that findings will be used increases if anthropologists collaborate with potential users.

____ 2.    Anthropologists today find fewer good field sites for research.

____ 3.    Anthropologists are interested in societies which have changed from tribal organization or food collecting to a market economy.

____ 4.    The Industrial Revolution had drastically negative effects on indigenous people.

____ 5.    Cultural data gathered on most peoples of the world is almost always accessible and understandable by nonanthropologists.

____ 6.    The discipline of anthropology is losing its subject matter.

____ 7.    Cultural Survival, Inc., works to guarantee the land and resource rights of tribal people while supporting economic development projects run by the people themselves.

____ 8.    Landless populations are forced to become laborers dependent upon wages.

____ 9.    Anthropologists are interested in the situation of the urban poor in the United States.

____ 10.    Even through fewer exist, cultural anthropologists' primary task is to continue to seek out and describe "uncontaminated" cultures of the world.

## SHORT ANSWER

1.    What will be the major differences between anthropological research in the future and that of the past?

2.    Why are anthropologists concerned about the survival of indigenous people?  What can they do to ensure their survival?

3.    Are anthropologists qualified to study complex societies?  What impact has the study of complex societies had on the research projects of anthropologists?

4.    What must anthropologist do to enable a wider use of the results of anthropological research

**ANSWER KEY**

## ANSWERS FOR CHAPTER 1

MULTIPLE CHOICE

| | | | | | | |
|---|---|---|---|---|---|---|
| 1. | A | 6. | B | 11. | C |
| 2. | A | 7. | D | 12. | D |
| 3. | D | 8. | A | 13. | B |
| 4. | B | 9. | C | 14. | C |
| 5. | B | 10. | D | 15. | A |

TRUE-FALSE

| | | | | | | |
|---|---|---|---|---|---|---|
| 1. | F | 8. | T | 15. | T |
| 2. | T | 9. | T | 16. | F |
| 3. | T | 10. | F | 17. | T |
| 4. | T | 11. | T | 18. | F |
| 5. | F | 12. | F | 19. | T |
| 6. | F | 13. | F | 20. | T |
| 7. | F | 14. | F | | |

MATCHING

| | | | | | | |
|---|---|---|---|---|---|---|
| 1. | C | 11. | A | 21. | A |
| 2. | C | 12. | B | 22. | B |
| 3. | C | 13. | A | 23. | A |
| 4. | D | 14. | C | 24. | A |
| 5. | B | 15. | C | 25. | B |
| 6. | C | 16. | A | 26. | B |
| 7. | D | 17. | B | 27. | B |
| 8. | B | 18. | A | 28. | B |
| 9. | C | 19. | B | 29. | B |
| 10. | C | 20. | B | 30. | A |

## ANSWERS FOR CHAPTER 2

MULTIPLE CHOICE

| | | | | | | | | |
|---|---|---|---|---|---|---|---|---|
| 1. | C | 6. | B | 11. | B | 16. | A |
| 2. | D | 7. | C | 12. | D | 17. | A |
| 3. | C | 8. | B | 13. | A | 18. | D |
| 4. | D | 9. | A | 14. | A | 19. | B |
| 5. | D | 10. | A | 15. | E | 20. | D |

TRUE-FALSE

| | | | | | | | | |
|---|---|---|---|---|---|---|---|---|
| 1. | F | 8. | F | 15. | F | 22. | F |
| 2. | T | 9. | T | 16. | T | 23. | T |
| 3. | F | 10. | T | 17. | T | 24. | F |
| 4. | F | 11. | F | 18. | T | 25. | T |
| 5. | T | 12. | F | 19. | T | | |
| 6. | T | 13. | F | 20. | T | | |
| 7. | T | 14. | T | 21. | F | | |

## ANSWERS FOR CHAPTER 3

MULTIPLE CHOICE

| | | | | | |
|---|---|---|---|---|---|
| 1. | C | 9. | D | 17. | C |
| 2. | B | 10. | D | 18. | D |
| 3. | A | 11. | B | 19. | B |
| 4. | D | 12. | A | 20 | A |
| 5. | C | 13. | C | 21. | A |
| 6. | B | 14. | D | 22. | A |
| 7. | A | 15. | B | 23. | A |
| 8. | E | 16. | E | 24. | C |

TRUE-FALSE

| | | | | | |
|---|---|---|---|---|---|
| 1. | T | 8. | F | 15. | T |
| 2. | T | 9. | T | 16. | F |
| 3. | F | 10. | F | 17. | F |
| 4. | F | 11. | F | 18. | F |
| 5. | T | 12. | T | 19. | F |
| 6. | F | 13. | T | 20. | T |
| 7. | F | 14. | T | | |

MATCHING

| | | | | | |
|---|---|---|---|---|---|
| 1. | G | 5. | K | 9. | C |
| 2. | D | 6. | A | 10. | F |
| 3. | B | 7. | E | 11. | J |
| 4. | H | 8. | I | | |

## ANSWERS TO CHAPTER 4

MULTIPLE CHOICE

| | | | | | |
|---|---|---|---|---|---|
| 1. | D | 9. | C | 17. | D |
| 2. | A | 10. | C | 18. | D |
| 3. | D | 11. | B | 19. | B |
| 4. | C | 12. | A | 20. | C |
| 5. | D | 13. | C | 21. | B |
| 6. | C | 14. | A | 22. | C |
| 7. | D | 15. | A | 23. | A |
| 8. | A | 16. | A | | |

TRUE-FALSE

| | | | | | |
|---|---|---|---|---|---|
| 1. | T | 9. | T | 17. | F |
| 2. | F | 10. | T | 18. | T |
| 3. | T | 11. | F | 19. | F |
| 4. | T | 12. | F | 20. | T |
| 5. | T | 13. | F | 21. | T |
| 6. | F | 14. | F | 22. | F |
| 7. | F | 15. | F | 23. | T |
| 8. | F | 16. | T | | |

MATCHING

| | | | | | | |
|---|---|---|---|---|---|---|
| 1. | H | 8. | E | 15. | I |
| 2. | D | 9. | B | 16. | A |
| 3. | E | 10. | H | 17. | L |
| 4. | F | 11. | B | 18. | D |
| 5. | E | 12. | C | 19. | L |
| 7. | J | 14. | L | | |

## ANSWERS FOR CHAPTER 5

MULTIPLE CHOICE

| | | | | | | |
|---|---|---|---|---|---|---|
| 1. | B | 8. | D | 15. | C |
| 2. | D | 9. | D | 16. | C |
| 3. | A | 10. | A | 17 | B |
| 4. | D | 11. | C | 18. | A |
| 5. | B | 12. | D | 19. | D |
| 6. | B | 13. | A | 20. | A |
| 7. | C | 14. | D | | |

TRUE-FALSE

| | | | | | | |
|---|---|---|---|---|---|---|
| 1. | T | 8. | F | 15. | F |
| 2. | T | 9. | F | 16. | F |
| 3. | F | 10. | T | 17. | F |
| 4. | T | 11. | F | 18. | F |
| 5. | T | 12. | T | 19. | F |
| 6. | T | 13. | T | 20. | T |
| 7. | F | 14. | F | | |

MATCHING

| | |
|---|---|
| 1. | F |
| 2. | B |
| 3. | E |
| 4. | C |
| 5. | A |
| 6. | D |

## ANSWERS FOR CHAPTER 6

MULTIPLE CHOICE

| | | | | | | |
|---|---|---|---|---|---|---|
| 1. | D | 8. | B | 15. | C |
| 2. | A | 9. | A | 16. | D |
| 3. | C | 10. | C | 17. | C |
| 4. | A | 11. | A | 18. | B |
| 5. | B | 12. | C | 19. | C |
| 6. | D | 13. | D | 20. | C |
| 7. | B | 14. | C | | |

TRUE-FALSE

| | | | | | |
|---|---|---|---|---|---|
| 1. | F | 8. | T | 15. | F |
| 2. | F | 9. | F | 16. | T |
| 3. | T | 10. | T | 17. | T |
| 4. | T | 11. | F | 18. | F |
| 5. | T | 12. | F | 19. | T |
| 6. | F | 13. | F | 20. | F |
| 7. | T | 14. | T | | |

## ANSWERS FOR CHAPTER 7

MULTIPLE CHOICE

| | | | | | |
|---|---|---|---|---|---|
| 1. | B | 7. | B | 13. | B |
| 2. | E | 8. | D | 14. | A |
| 3. | B | 9. | B | 15. | D |
| 4. | D | 10. | D | 16. | B |
| 5. | D | 11. | E | 17. | D |
| 6. | C | 12. | A | 18. | B |

TRUE-FALSE

| | | | | | |
|---|---|---|---|---|---|
| 1. | T | 9. | T | 17. | T |
| 2. | F | 10. | F | 18. | F |
| 3. | T | 11. | F | 19. | T |
| 4. | F | 12. | T | 20. | T |
| 5. | T | 13. | F | 21. | T |
| 6. | F | 14. | F | 22. | F |
| 7. | F | 15. | F | | |
| 8. | F | 16. | T | | |

MATCHING

| | | | |
|---|---|---|---|
| 1. | E | 6. | A |
| 2. | B | 7. | E |
| 3. | B | 8. | D |
| 4. | C | 9. | A |
| 5. | C | 10. | E |

## ANSWERS FOR CHAPTER 8

MULTIPLE CHOICE

| | | | | | |
|---|---|---|---|---|---|
| 1. | D | 8. | C | 15. | B |
| 2. | D | 9. | E | 16. | C |
| 3. | D | 10. | D | 17. | D |
| 4. | A | 11. | B | 18. | C |
| 5. | D | 12. | B | 19. | B |
| 6. | E | 13. | E | 20. | B |
| 7. | C | 14. | D | | |

TRUE-FALSE

| | | | | | | |
|---|---|---|---|---|---|
| 1. | T | 9. | F | 17. | T |
| 2. | T | 10. | F | 18. | F |
| 3. | T | 11. | F | 19. | T |
| 4. | F | 12. | F | 20. | T |
| 5. | F | 13. | T | 21. | T |
| 6. | T | 14. | T | 22. | F |
| 7. | T | 15. | T | | |
| 8. | T | 16. | F | | |

## ANSWERS FOR CHAPTER 9

MULTIPLE CHOICE

| | | | | | | |
|---|---|---|---|---|---|
| 1. | D | 8. | C | 15. | C |
| 2. | D | 9. | C | 16. | D |
| 3. | B | 10. | D | 17. | D |
| 4. | B | 11. | B | 18. | C |
| 5. | A | 12. | B | 19. | B |
| 6. | B | 13. | D | 20. | D |
| 7. | B | 14. | A | | |

TRUE-FALSE

| | | | | | | |
|---|---|---|---|---|---|
| 1. | T | 8. | T | 15. | F |
| 2. | F | 9. | T | 16. | F |
| 3. | T | 10. | F | 17. | T |
| 4. | F | 11. | T | 18. | T |
| 5. | T | 12. | T | 19. | T |
| 6. | F | 13. | F | 20. | F |
| 7. | F | 14. | F | | |

## ANSWERS FOR CHAPTER 10

MULTIPLE CHOICE

| | | | | | | |
|---|---|---|---|---|---|
| 1. | A | 8. | B | 15. | A |
| 2. | B | 9. | E | 16. | D |
| 3. | B | 10. | C | 17. | A |
| 4. | C | 11. | C | 18. | B |
| 5. | D | 12. | B | 19. | E |
| 6. | B | 13. | C | 20. | D |
| 7. | C | 14. | D | | |

TRUE-FALSE

| | | | | | | |
|---|---|---|---|---|---|
| 1. | T | 8. | F | 15. | F |
| 2. | T | 9. | F | 16. | T |
| 3. | F | 10. | T | 17. | T |
| 4. | T | 11. | T | 18. | F |
| 5. | F | 12. | F | 19. | F |
| 6. | F | 13. | F | 20. | T |
| 7. | T | 14. | T | | |

MATCHING

| | | | | |
|---|---|---|---|---|
| 1. | E | 6. | A | |
| 2. | B | 7. | C | |
| 3. | D | 8. | I | |
| 4. | G | 9. | F | |
| 5. | H | 10. | J | |

## ANSWERS FOR CHAPTER 11

MULTIPLE CHOICE

| | | | | | |
|---|---|---|---|---|---|
| 1. | D | 8. | A | 15. | C |
| 2. | E | 9. | C | 16. | B |
| 3. | C | 10. | C | 17. | B |
| 4. | D | 11. | D | 18. | B |
| 5. | B | 12. | B | 19. | A |
| 6. | D | 13. | D | 20. | A |
| 7. | D | 14. | A | | |

TRUE-FALSE

| | | | | | |
|---|---|---|---|---|---|
| 1. | F | 8. | F | 15. | F |
| 2. | F | 9. | T | 16. | T |
| 3. | F | 10. | T | 17. | T |
| 4. | F | 11. | F | 18. | T |
| 5. | T | 12. | T | 19. | T |
| 6. | T | 13. | T | 20. | T |
| 7. | T | 14. | T | | |

## ANSWERS FOR CHAPTER 12

MULTIPLE CHOICE

| | | | | | |
|---|---|---|---|---|---|
| 1. | C | 8. | D | 15. | C |
| 2. | D | 9. | A | 16. | B |
| 3. | A | 10. | D | 17. | B |
| 4. | C | 11. | A | 18. | B |
| 5. | D | 12. | D | 19. | A |
| 6. | A | 13. | B | 20. | D |
| 7. | D | 14. | C | | |

TRUE-FALSE

| | | | | | |
|---|---|---|---|---|---|
| 1. | T | 8. | T | 15. | F |
| 2. | F | 9. | T | 16. | T |
| 3. | F | 10. | T | 17. | F |
| 4. | T | 11. | F | 18. | T |
| 5. | F | 12. | T | 19. | T |
| 6. | T | 13. | T | 20. | T |
| 7. | T | 14. | T | | |

MATCHING

| | | | | |
|---|---|---|---|---|
| 1. | C | 6. | D | |
| 2. | A | 7. | D | |
| 3. | D | 8. | A | |
| 4. | C | 9. | B | |
| 5. | B | 10. | C | |

## ANSWERS FOR CHAPTER 13

MULTIPLE CHOICE

| | | | | | | |
|---|---|---|---|---|---|---|
| 1. | D | 8. | C | 15. | D |
| 2. | A | 9. | D | 16. | A |
| 3. | C | 10. | C | 17. | D |
| 4. | C | 11. | B | 18. | B |
| 5. | A | 12. | D | 19. | D |
| 6. | A | 13. | C | 20. | A |
| 7. | B | 14. | A | | |

TRUE-FALSE

| | | | | | | |
|---|---|---|---|---|---|---|
| 1. | F | 8. | T | 15. | T |
| 2. | T | 9. | T | 16. | T |
| 3. | F | 10. | T | 17. | F |
| 4. | T | 11. | T | 18. | T |
| 5. | F | 12. | T | 19. | T |
| 6. | T | 13. | T | 20. | T |
| 7. | T | 14. | T | | |

## ANSWERS TO CHAPTER 14

MULTIPLE CHOICE

| | | | | | | |
|---|---|---|---|---|---|---|
| 1. | D | 8. | C | 15. | E |
| 2. | D | 9. | A | 16. | B |
| 3. | E | 10. | B | 17 | C |
| 4. | C | 11. | A | 18. | B |
| 5. | B | 12. | B | 19. | C |
| 6. | C | 13. | A | 20. | D |
| 7. | A | 14. | B | | |

TRUE-FALSE

| | | | | | | |
|---|---|---|---|---|---|---|
| 1. | T | 8. | F | 15. | F |
| 2. | F | 9. | T | 16. | T |
| 3. | F | 10. | T | 17. | T |
| 4. | T | 11. | T | 18. | T |
| 5. | F | 12. | T | 19. | F |
| 6. | T | 13. | T | 20. | T |
| 7. | F | 14. | T | | |

MATCHING

| | | | |
|---|---|---|---|
| 1. | B | 6. | B |
| 2. | A | 7. | B |
| 3. | B | 8. | A |
| 4. | D | 9. | D |
| 5. | D | 10. | C |

## ANSWERS FOR CHAPTER 15

MULTIPLE CHOICE

| | | | | | |
|---|---|---|---|---|---|
| 1. | D | 8. | A | 15. | C |
| 2. | C | 9. | E | 16. | D |
| 3. | B | 10. | D | 17. | C |
| 4. | C | 11. | D | 18. | A |
| 5. | C | 12. | D | 19. | D |
| 6. | D | 13. | C | 20. | C |
| 7. | D | 14. | D | | |

TRUE-FALSE

| | | | | | |
|---|---|---|---|---|---|
| 1. | F | 8. | T | 15. | F |
| 2. | T | 9. | F | 16. | T |
| 3. | T | 10. | T | 17. | F |
| 4. | F | 11. | F | 18. | T |
| 5. | T | 12. | F | 19. | T |
| 6. | T | 13. | F | 20. | F |
| 7. | F | 14. | T | | |

## ANSWERS FOR CHAPTER 16

MULTIPLE CHOICE

| | | | | | |
|---|---|---|---|---|---|
| 1. | C | 8. | D | 15. | C |
| 2. | A | 9. | B | 16. | C |
| 3. | C | 10. | B | 17. | D |
| 4. | C | 11. | C | 18. | A |
| 5. | D | 12. | D | 19. | C |
| 6. | D | 13. | E | 20. | A |
| 7. | D | 14. | A | | |

TRUE-FALSE

| | | | | | |
|---|---|---|---|---|---|
| 1. | T | 8. | T | 15. | T |
| 2. | F | 9. | T | 16. | T |
| 3. | F | 10. | F | 17. | T |
| 4. | T | 11. | F | 18. | T |
| 5. | T | 12. | T | 19. | T |
| 6. | F | 13. | T | 20. | T |
| 7. | T | 14. | T | | |

## ANSWERS FOR CHAPTER 17

MULTIPLE CHOICE

| | | | | | |
|---|---|---|---|---|---|
| 1. | D | 7. | B | 13. | A |
| 2. | C | 8. | D | 14. | D |
| 3. | D | 9. | D | 15. | C |
| 4. | C | 10. | E | 16. | B |
| 5. | D | 11. | D | 17. | A |
| 6. | D | 12. | B | 18. | A |

TRUE-FALSE

| | | | |
|---|---|---|---|
| 1. | T | 6. | F |
| 2. | F | 7. | T |
| 3. | T | 8. | T |
| 4. | T | 9. | T |
| 5. | F | 10. | F |